high protein vegan

hearty whole food meals, raw desserts and more

Hildajorgensen@live.com

http://highproteinvegan.wordpress.com

1. introduction

2. meals in minutes

3. meal salads, and high raw meals

4. stews, soups, curries and other stovetop meals

about the recipe symbols

GF Gluten-Free. These recipes contain no gluten or oats. If you are avoiding gluten but oats are not a problem, then all recipes in this book, with the exception of chapters 8 and 9 are suitable if the right ingredients are chosen.

   Soy-free. All the recipes in this book can be made soy-free, provided that ingredients such as miso and vegan worcestershire sauce are free from soy. While miso is typically thought of as a soy food, several brands of chickpea-based miso are becoming more readily available and are usually soy-free. Adzuki bean miso can also be found online.

NSI No Specialty Ingredients. All the ingredients needed for these recipes can be found in a typical supermarket.

LF Low fat. These recipes contain less than 1 teaspoon of fat per serve.

NF Nightshade-Free. These recipes do not contain any potatoes, tomatoes, capsicums, chillis or eggplants.

OGF Onion- and Garlic-Free. These recipes contain no ingredients from the onion and garlic family of vegetables.

NN No Nuts. These recipes contain no peanuts or tree nuts.

Under 45 minutes These recipes take less than 45 minutes in total, including preparation time.

When cooking for people with allergies be sure to check the ingredients list of any pre-made products used, such as vegan milk, sauces and baking powder, to ensure they are suitable.

about the recipes

The recipes in this book have been designed to be high in protein, filling and nutritious. While some of the recipes in chapters 2 to 9 don't need anything to complete them as a full meal (although a simple raw salad will complement most of them), other recipes only constitute the protein portion of a meal, and to create a balanced meal from them it is recommended that they be served with carbohydrate-rich food such as starchy vegetables or grains. The photographs accompanying the recipes will typically show whether anything else is needed to complete the meal, or it will be written in the recipe introduction or instructions.

"where do you get your protein?"

From hearing this question so often we might gather that protein is a mysterious substance which is difficult to find in the vegan diet, but protein can actually be found in most foods. Protein is comprised of 20 amino acids, the human body can produce 11 of these and for optimum health the remaining 9 need to be gained from food. These 9 amino acids are called essential amino acids.

Complete proteins contain good amounts of all 9 essential amino acids. Vegan complete proteins include soy and quinoa. It is easy to get the right balance of essential aminos without eating either quinoa or soy - and all the recipes in this book have a soy-free option.

Lysine is an essential amino acid which is high in legumes such as beans, lentils and peas, but low in most other vegan foods. Legumes contain lower amounts of the essential aminos methionine and tryptophan, and this can be balanced out by eating vegetables, grains, nuts and seeds - something which usually isn't an issue for vegans.

New research has shown that contrary to an established belief from the 1970s it is not necessary to eat high amounts of all the essential aminos in one meal to get the right balance of amino acids. If a variety of foods are eaten throughout the day then the body is able to find the right amount of all the essential aminos.

The need for protein in the diet has been estimated to be around 0.9g per kilogram (0.015oz per pound) of body weight. This amount increases for those who are pregnant, breastfeeding, on low calorie diets, recovering from injuries, involved in athletics or strength training, ranging from 1.1g per kilogram of weight for pregnancy through to two to three grams per kilogram for strength training. For those who are overweight, protein per kilogram of body weight is calculated by the healthy weight for their height, so they may find that they need less than 0.9g per kilogram of their present body weight. These are only estimates, and the need for protein varies from person to person with some people being happy on diets relatively low in protein, and others feeling that low protein food isn't filling enough for them, and need to eat higher protein meals and snacks in order to feel satisfied.

For children the estimated protein requirements are calculated by age, rather than weight.

designing a protein-rich meal

If you often use canned beans it can be useful to base meals around the one and a half cups of beans that come in 14oz (400g) tins. In general around three quarters of a cup of cooked legumes per serving is a good amount for those with higher protein needs, with half a cup being enough for those with average protein requirements.

To determine whether a recipe is high in protein, ask:
•Does it involve many legumes, nuts or seeds?
•Is there a way I can add legumes, nuts or seeds to the dish while still being able to enjoy it as much as before?

However, if you need a high protein meal but still want to enjoy a low protein dish without changing it at all:

Add legumes, nuts and seeds to side dishes
If you suspect that your main dish might be too low in protein for your needs, then it's easy enough to make a side dish with extra protein. Sprinkle seeds, nuts and beans over a salad or as a small side dish on their own. Choose chickpea chips (page 46) instead of hot potato chips as a side dish. Pappadams are made from ground legumes so can add extra protein to an Indian meal, along with a delicious crunchy element that can turn a simple curry and rice meal into something special. Cannellini beans and other white beans can be mashed with potatoes for a side dish that is higher in protein than plain mashed potatoes.

Choose higher-protein grains
Quinoa is a nutritious grain which is high in protein and contains good amounts of all the essential amino acids. It also cooks up a lot faster than other whole grains. Try replacing rice with quinoa or amaranth for extra protein.

High protein desserts
Raw desserts are often high in nuts and seeds, and as a result high in protein. Chickpea flour can be a great high-protein addition to baked goods, it works well as an egg replacer (use 1/4 cup chickpea flour and 1/4 cup water for every egg called for in a recipe), and can also be substituted for some of the other flours called for in recipes (although you may find the texture is denser than the original recipe, and will require a slightly longer cooking time).

High Protein Drinks
Soy milk, along with homemade nut and seed milks tend to have the highest amount of protein per serve compared to other vegan milks such as coconut, rice and oat milk.

more essential information about vegan nutrition

I haven't provided calorie counts or detailed nutritional information for any of the recipes because I don't believe these can provide an accurate reflection on the qualities of a vegan wholefoods recipe. Reducing nutrition to numerical value results in homegrown vegetables being put on the same level as the products of industrial agriculture. With some research it's easy enough to tell the nutritional value of a recipe by looking at an ingredients list. I also don't wish to ruin the magic of cooking by making it overly scientific. While this book focuses on high protein meals, the protein content of many recipes will vary depending on which legume is used - I'd prefer for a recipe to be flexible and easy to adapt to whatever ingredients are on hand than to have a protein count next to the recipe. That being said, there are a few things to watch out for in the vegan diet. I will not go into every nutrient that humans need, but will point out a few things that vegans need to be especially aware of. If you're eating a colourful variety of fruit and vegetables, including plenty of leafy greens, chances are that you're getting most of the nutrients you need. Here is a list of some nutrients that vegans sometimes struggle with, and how to counter that without resorting to synthetic vitamin pills.

Raw and Lightly Cooked Foods

I recommend serving most meals from this book with a raw side salad, or some lightly cooked greens. Many people overcook vegetables. I like to steam or sauté side-serves of vegetables until they're just cooked, but still crunchy. You can tell this by the change in colour in the vegetables. For example, when steaming or boiling broccoli, finish cooking as soon as the colour changes to a vibrant green. This only takes about two minutes. If you leave the steaming or sautéing until everything else in the meal is ready, then you have more chance of success with this, and ultimately more nutrients and texture. Adding raw and lightly cooked foods to meals not only provides a greater variety and quality of nutrients, but adds interest to a meal, with lighter, crunchier bites in between tastes of 'heavier' foods like seitan and legume dishes. It's as easy as making a garden salad or adding some raw kale to each plate of stew.

Vitamin B12 is something many vegans need to be aware of. If you cook with plenty of nutritional yeast (savoury yeast flakes) a couple of times a week, or regularly sprinkle it on your meals then you're probably getting enough of this in your diet. It is also sometimes found in fortified vegan milks. If you're not confident that you're getting it from these sources, then it may be a good idea to supplement with tablets. If you're relying on nutritional yeast for vitamin b12 intake, be sure to check that the kind you're using contains it, as some nutritional yeasts do not have any b12.

Iodine can be found in sea vegetables; it is especially high in kelp, which is best bought in granule form to add nutrition to savoury dishes; it also adds depth to the flavours when used in small amounts, without making your food taste like sea vegetables. A small amount is all that is needed if eaten every day. I haven't included it as an ingredient in all my recipes because I don't wish to over-complicate things, but I would recommend adding a pinch of kelp granules per serve to any savoury meal once a day, especially if you are pregnant or breastfeeding.

Vitamin D is essential for calcium absorption. There are two forms of it: D2 and D3. D2 can be found in mushrooms that have been exposed to the sun, as well as in a few vegan supplements. D3 can be absorbed by exposure to direct sunlight (the amount of sunlight exposure needed depends on your location and your body's ability to absorb D3 from sunlight), and also (as of 2012) is available in a vegan supplement called Vitashine. Some sources state that D2 is not as readily absorbed as D3, and that higher doses of D2 can be dangerous, while others believe that there is no difference in absorption and safety.

Calcium can be found in naturally high levels in certain sea vegetables, particularly lithothamnium cacareum (sold by some companies as 'natural calcium' 'green calcium' 'ocean calcium' and 'organic calcium'), or as Aquamin, which is sometimes added to vegan milks. Many nuts, seeds, beans and vegetables such as collards, kale and broccoli have high levels of calcium.

Fats, and the essential fatty acids Omega 3 and 6

Fat is necessary for the human body to absorb vitamins and function healthily. It also contributes to a balanced meal by adding flavour along with providing sustained energy to keep the eater full for longer. Weight gain is caused by an excess of unused energy from food and can be fixed by using this energy for physical activity. I have included a low fat category in this book not because I believe a low fat diet is beneficial for all people, but to make it easier for people who are already on low fat diets to find suitable recipes.

Omega 3 and 6 are found in some kinds of fat, and it's important to have a good balance between these. The modern diet is often very high in polyunsaturated oils which contain a lot of omega 6, with low levels of omega 3, and for the best health it is a good idea to correct this. A good balance can be obtained by eating chia seeds, flaxseeds, hempseeds, walnuts and their cold-pressed oils to get extra omega 3, along with limiting your intake of oils which are high in omega 6.

To limit your intake of omega 6, it's best to use cold-pressed olive oil and coconut oil in place of other oils whenever possible. These are minimally processed oils that have been used traditionally for a long time and are much lower in omega 6 than other oils like sunflower, safflower and canola.

8 Flaxseed oil and ground flaxseeds go rancid at room temperature, so if you are buying these make sure they are refrigerated, and that the flaxseed oil is cold-processed.

The Best Oils for Cooking, and Oils to Avoid

Cold-pressed olive oil is delicious both in salad dressings and in cooking. This oil has been used for thousands of years, and is a good choice if you only have one oil in the kitchen.

Olive oil can be replaced with safflower or sunflower oils for those looking for a cheaper alternative. These oils have not had as much traditional use as olive oil, and are high in omega 6, so it's important if you are using a lot of these oils to be eating plenty of foods high in omega 3, such as chia seeds, flaxseeds, walnuts and hemp seeds, to correct the balance.

There has been some debate over how oils handle the high temperatures involved in cooking, and much of this argument is in favour of coconut oil for use in baked dishes. Coconut oil solidifies at a cold room temperature, making it ideal for replacing butter and margarine. To work with cold coconut oil, you'll first need to melt it by placing the jar of it in a larger bowl filled with hot water, so that the jar stands up and isn't on its side (water can leak into the jar if it falls over). If you need a larger amount of coconut oil, you will need to use boiling water or leave the jar to sit for a longer time. Refined coconut oil goes through a process of being filtered through clay to remove the scent and taste of coconut, making it a good choice for all kinds of dishes that you don't wish to taste of coconut.

For those avoiding genetically modified foods, the cooking oils that are usually genetically modified are canola (rapeseed), cottonseed, corn and soya. These are best replaced by olive oil.

Iron and Zinc

Getting enough iron for most vegans is not an issue at all. High levels can be found in leafy green vegetables, and cooking in cast iron cookware will also result in a high iron intake. Vitamin C is important for iron absorption, and this can often be found in the same vegetables that contain iron, or in fruits and apple cider vinegar. Legumes such as lentils, chickpeas and cannellini beans are another good source of iron, along with dark chocolate and a number of other delicious vegan foods. So if you are adding leafy greens to your meals or having at least one side-dish salad a day you should have no problems with this. ZInc is generally found in the same vegetable sources as iron, so deficiency in this is usually not an issue in a healthy vegan wholefoods diet. Pumpkin seeds are also great source of zinc, so for those worried about zinc intake it can be a good idea to sprinkle meals with pumpkin seeds.

Avoiding GMOs

Many people are concerned about the impacts genetically modified foods have on their health, and the health of future generations. Genetically modified crops are often engineered to withstand high doses of herbicides, or to create their own pesticide, and even as I write crops are being developed for the most cosmetic and unnatural of reasons, and not with our health in mind. Given that the methods used to grow genetically modified crops end up with the local wildlife and ecosystems being poisoned, it really goes against vegan ethics to be eating these crops.

Avoiding these products on an unprocessed wholefoods diet is easy, and only a matter of finding out which genetically modified crops are grown in which area, so you can be sure that by avoiding these products you are avoiding genetically modified food. Currently (2012) all organically certified products must be completely free of GMOs, so by making sure the sources of these products are organic, you are also avoiding GMOs. Many countries also have organisations around to help people avoid GMOs; for instance, in Australia there is the True Food Network, which publishes lists of companies which are boycotting GMOs, so you can be sure that if you are buying non-organic food, you are not supporting genetic engineering. Sometimes in processed foods the genetically modified oils (corn, cottonseed, soybean and canola) are simply labeled "vegetable oil". This book will help you to avoid GMOs by providing you with ideas and recipes for delicious meals and treats which can easily be fitted into busy lives, to reduce or completely eliminate dependence on processed food and takeaways.

sprouting beans

A couple of the recipes in this book call for sprouted mung beans. To sprout, first rinse then soak the mung beans for 8-12 hours at room temperature in cold water. Drain and rinse, then place the beans in a nutmilk bag or cloth inside a colander, or other container which will allow the beans to drain. Cover and leave to sit at room temperature for around 8-12 hours, then rinse and leave to drain again.

Continue to rinse and leave the beans to drain 2-3 times every 24 hours. The beans will be ready to eat in 2-3 more days, when there are sprouts growing out of them. The sprouts can continue to grow and be eaten for up to a week. If you wish to stop the growth, simply place them in the fridge and eat them within a few days.

recommended ingredients

Apple cider vinegar, balsamic vinegar and red wine vinegar.

Oils (Cold-pressed olive and coconut are the most important, see page 9).

Salt - The less refined, the better. Salts that have a colour, smell and nice taste, such as Celtic sea salt, Himalayan crystal salt, fleur de sel and Victorian lake salt are the best choices. If you're using a refined salt you may need to reduce the amount of salt called for in these recipes, as refined salts contain higher amounts of sodium, fewer other minerals and the flavour isn't as pleasant.

Miso and/or tamari, shoyu or coconut aminos - Fermented condiments for adding delicious savoury flavours to food.

Vegan worcestershire sauce - Some worcestershire sauces contain fish, so be sure to check the ingredients. If it is labeled 'suitable for vegetarians', this will generally mean that it's OK for vegans too.

Tomato sauce or ketchup - I like to use sauces which are thick and bright, but not overly sweet. The more watery, chutney-style tomato sauces won't work so well in my recipes, so it's worth getting a more concentrated, ketchup-style sauce for cooking, even if you don't like the taste of it on its own.

Chickpea flour - a high protein flour that is great for replacing eggs, making soy-free tofu and for increasing the protein in baked goods. Also known as besan flour, cici flour, chana flour, gram flour and garbanzo bean flour, it can be found in health food shops, along with Indian, Italian and French grocery shops.

Gluten (vital wheat gluten) - For the seitan dishes.

Nutritional yeast (savoury yeast flakes) - This is high in protein and essential for creating a 'cheese' flavour in dishes, along with adding extra savoury flavour and nutrition. It's worth tracking down over the internet if you can't find it in shops.

Wholemeal wheat flour, or wholemeal spelt flour - For yeast bread baking.

Barley flour, wholewheat pastry flour or wholemeal spelt flour - These are low gluten flours for baking sweet food, but can also be used for pretty much any purpose where flour is called for, except for making yeast breads. Barley flour is the best of these, and you may find that you need to use a teaspoon or two of extra water per cup of flour if you're using spelt or wholewheat pastry flour.

Rolled oats, steamed oats or quick oats.

Nuts - Cashews, walnuts, almonds.

Nut butters - High protein spreads for bread, and for use in raw desserts. Peanut and almond are recommended, although only used in a couple of the recipes in this book.

Seeds - Sunflower, pumpkin and sesame.

Grains - Brown rice and quinoa.

Lentils - Red split and whole brown/green ones.

Canned or dried beans - Chickpeas, adzuki beans, cannellini beans, butter beans or lima beans, borlotti or pinto beans, black beans, dried mung beans (for sprouting).

Tomato purée, canned tomatoes, or fresh tomatoes.

Wholemeal spaghetti and penne.

Tahini (sesame seed paste) - unhulled is the best, but harder to find than the hulled version.

Dijon mustard.

Organic cornmeal (polenta).

Dried or fresh herbs - Most of these recipes call for dried herbs, rather than fresh, these can be replaced by fresh herbs by using 2-4 times the amount called for, and adding it towards the end of the cooking rather than at the start. Oregano, thyme, sage and rosemary are the most important in this cookbook.

Spices - Cayenne pepper, coriander, cumin, cloves, black pepper, mustard seeds (yellow and brown), turmeric, garam masala, paprika, smoked paprika, fennel seeds, nutmeg and cinnamon.

Cacao or cocoa powder.

Rapadura, sucanat, coconut sugar or raw sugar - Rapadura, sucanat and coconut sugar are the healthier choices of these sugars, but more expensive and harder to find. To turn into caster sugar or powdered sugar, grind in a food processor or coffee grinder, adding a teaspoon of tapioca flour per cup for powdered sugar. These sugars work just as well in sweet dishes as the refined stuff, which is sometimes processed using animal products.

Barley malt syrup, molasses or golden syrup.

Vanilla extract - The best stuff will be labeled 'natural' and contains real vanilla.

Vanilla beans - For use in some raw desserts - slice lengthways through the centre of the bean and scrape out all the black pulp for use in recipes.

Agave syrup - For use in some raw desserts. I recommend using a high quality dark raw agave syrup such as Loving Earth.

Medjool dates - For raw desserts. Other kinds of soft dates can be substituted.

Bicarb soda (sodium bicarbonate).

vegetables and fruit

Garlic - Local and organic is best, imported garlic is often bleached, irradiated and sprayed with chemicals.

Ginger - This will keep for a while if you keep it in open air, it's good to have on hand if you often make Indian food.

Onions or leeks.

Spring onions (green onions) are useful in a couple of the recipes from this book.

Salad greens (lettuce, mesclun, red Russian or Tuscan kale, red cabbage).

Cooking greens (e.g. kale, silverbeet (swiss chard), collards, spinach).

Cauliflower.

Broccoli.

Potatoes or swedes (rutabagas).

Sweet potatoes.

Carrots.

Butternut pumpkin.

Lemons.

Bananas - for some raw desserts.

cooking grains and beans

* When using canned beans, always drain and thoroughly rinse the beans before adding them to the recipe.

* All lentils called for in these recipes are measured dry, and the cooking times taken into account in the recipe. To speed up cooking times in some recipes you could use tinned brown lentils instead, giving a few more under 45 minute options.

* Never add salt to the cooking water of dry beans or lentils until they are cooked.

* Beans are generally measured in their cooked amounts. A 400g (14oz) tin is 1 1/2 cups of cooked beans.

cooking grains

To cook any grain, you first need to rinse it in cold water, then briefly drain. Put the grain and the required amount of cold water to a saucepan and bring it to the boil on a medium-high setting with the lid on. Once it is thoroughly boiling, reduce the heat to a low setting and simmer for the time specified.

For quinoa: 15 minutes. 1 part quinoa to 2 parts water. (or 1 part quinoa to 1 3/4 parts water if the quinoa has been soaked for 8 hours beforehand)
For amaranth: 20 minutes. 1 part amaranth to 2 1/2 parts water.
For brown rice: 25-30 minutes. 1 part brown rice to 1 1/2 parts water.
For barley: 30-40 minutes. 1 part barley to 2 parts water.

Take the pan off the heat and leave it to sit with the lid on for 5-10 minutes to finish cooking.

Try not to take the lid off at all during the cooking process, as this will result in more of the water evaporating, and less soaking into the grains. Grains cooked this way do not need stirring during the cooking time.

soaking and cooking beans

Quick soaking: Rinse the beans, then bring them and at least triple the amount of water to the boil. Boil rapidly for 2 minutes, then turn the heat off and leave for an hour with the lid on.

Overnight soaking: Rinse the beans and place in a bowl with at least three times their height in cold water. Leave to sit at room temperature for 8-24 hours.

Cooking:
When the beans have finished soaking, drain and rinse. Cover with at least twice their height in cold water and bring to the boil. Boil rapidly for 3 minutes, then reduce the heat and simmer for the specified time. The times will vary depending on how long the beans have been soaked, their age, and how they've been stored.

Chickpeas: 1-2 hours
Borlotti beans: 1-2 hours
Red Kidney beans: 1- 2 hours
Adzuki Beans: 45 - 90 minutes
Cannellini beans: 45-90 minutes
Black (turtle) beans: 45-60 minutes
Butter beans (lima beans): 1 - 1 1/2 hours
Split red lentils (no soaking required): 10-20 minutes
Whole brown/green lentils (no soaking required): 30-45 minutes
French puy lentils (black lentils) (no soaking required): 40-50 minutes

* Beans and lentils generally swell to 2 1/2 to 3 times their dry size once cooked. To cook enough beans to replace a 400g (14oz) tin, soak and cook 2/3 cup of dry beans, and you will have at least 1 1/2 cups of cooked beans.

* If dark froth develops on the surface of the water during cooking, discard as much of the froth as possible by skimming it off with a spoon.

understanding umami, and how to cook to impress anyone

Any vegan who has discussed veganism with sympathetic non-vegans has most likely encountered something along the lines of "I'd like to go vegan, but I'd miss cheese too much". Animal products generally contain a lot of umami flavours, so many people having only been exposed to vegan food low in umami assume that they will have to go without umami flavours in order to be on a vegan diet. With some understanding, along with a few key ingredients and techniques vegan meals can be hearty and savoury enough impress anyone.

Umami is a Japanese word, which translates as "pleasant savoury taste". It is a distinct taste that the human tongue has receptors for, and it can be found in many vegan foods, especially fermented ones.

If you taste your food towards the end of the cooking time and feel that it needs a little extra 'something', that 'something' could be umami. Instead of adding salt, try adding a little miso, tamari, nutritional yeast or coconut aminos. Adding a little vinegar to dishes also helps to enhance the flavours, balsamic vinegar is the highest in umami.

Other rich sources of umami include nutritional yeast, sea vegetables, tomatoes, olives, mushrooms, saurkraut and pickled vegetables.

Any vegetable that has been browned by sautéing, roasting, grilling or broiling is going to be higher in umami than a raw, steamed or boiled vegetable. Many of my stovetop recipes begin with sautéing onions in a little hot olive oil for this purpose.

While a vegan meal doesn't need any of these ingredients in order to be tasty, if you are wanting to impress someone that usually eats a lot of animal foods or claims to not enjoy vegan food, it can be a good idea to serve food with plenty of umami flavour.

cooking tips

Always make sure the oven is fully preheated before starting to bake anything.

Many of my savoury dishes involve sautéing. For best results heat two to three teaspoons of oil in the pan, then add the onion once the pan and the oil have heated up. You should be able to tell when it's hot enough by how quickly the oil moves around the pan when tipped. If it is slow then it's not ready, but once it is fast and the oil appears to be thinner than it was when cold, then it is probably ready. Test this by sprinkling a tiny bit of water in with your hands; if it quickly sizzles, then it's time to add the onion. Add the onion to this, usually at a medium-high heat, and stir it around, coating it in the oil. Continue to stir for a little longer. For the best results stir it frequently until the onion has coloured up and is tender and smells tasty, which should only take a couple of minutes.

To shallow fry, heat the specified amount of oil (usually around 1/4-1/2 cm (1/8-1/4")) in a frying pan over medium-high heat. Tilt the pan around slightly as it heats up and note when it starts to move more freely. Test by placing a small piece of whatever you are cooking in the oil; it should sizzle straight away when it's ready.

Most stovetop dishes are generally cooked with the lids on when left to simmer. This results in faster cooking, and in more predictable results when cooking grains. If you don't have lids, you could cover the saucepans with plates.

Kale is always used with the stem ripped off. To do this quickly, hold the stem in one hand and run your other hand along the edges, ripping off the leafy parts.

Home cooked beans taste a lot better than canned beans, are cheaper and use less packaging. Try soaking and cooking up a big batch of a particular bean and using the index of this book to find suitable recipes to use it in.

Quinoa is best thoroughly rinsed before cooking. To rinse quinoa place it in a bowl, fill the bowl up with lukewarm water and mix with your fingers to try and remove as much of the bitter-tasting coating as possible. Drain and repeat twice, then drain again. For the best tasting quinoa, soak it in some fresh cold water for 8-24 hours, drain and then cook, using a little less water than you would for unsoaked quinoa.

While measuring cups don't tend to have too much variation, for the best results with these recipes I recommend using the standard US measuring cup volume of 235ml (8oz).

meals in minutes

wholesome meals, complete in less than 30 minutes

omelette

These are a very quick and easy dish to make. In the photo the omelette is stuffed with kale, tomatoes and homemade cashew cheese, but all kinds of toppings are great on these omelettes. I often eat them stuffed with pickled gherkin slices and kale. For a filling meal serve them with cooked grains, bread, oven chips or roasted vegetables.

Gluten-Free, Soy-Free,
Low Fat, Nightshade-Free,
Onion- and Garlic-Free, No Nuts
Under 45 minutes
Total time: 20 minutes
Serves 2

ingredients

1 cup chickpea flour
3 tablespoons nutritional yeast (savoury yeast flakes)
1/2-1 teaspoon salt
1 teaspoon cracked pepper
1 cup water

method

Combine the chickpea flour, nutritional yeast, salt and pepper in a mixing bowl, breaking up any lumps. Add the water a little at a time, mixing to form a batter.

Thoroughly brush or spray a frying pan with olive oil and heat on a medium-high setting. When the pan is hot, pour in half the batter (if it is thicker in the centre and thinner on the outside you can use the back of a metal spoon to gently spread the batter out).

Cook without disturbing until the edges are cooked through and there are bubbles in the middle. Gently flip over and cook for a further minute or two, until the other side is completely cooked. Place on a plate, keeping it warm in the oven if you wish.

When the first omelette is out of the pan, quickly pour the other half of the batter in and cook in the same way.

Put toppings on one half of each circle and flip the other side over the top.

omelette florentine

The classic combination of greens and a subtly flavoured creamy sauce, served on top of a vegan omelette and a slice of bread. I like to sauté the greens with some onions for extra flavour, but they can also be steamed for this recipe.

Gluten-Free Option,
Nightshade-Free
Onion- and Garlic-Free Option
No Nuts, Under 45 minutes
Kitchen time: 25 minutes
Serves 2

ingredients

For the sauce:
3 tablespoons wholegrain flour
1 tablespoon nutritional yeast (savoury yeast flakes)
3 tablespoons olive oil
1 cup vegan milk or water
1/2-1 teaspoon apple cider vinegar or lemon juice
1/4 teaspoon salt
optional pinch of nutmeg

For the greens and onions:
2 teaspoons olive oil
half a medium onion, finely chopped
a pinch of salt
6 large leaves kale, silverbeet or chard (or 4-5 cups spinach leaves)

2 large slices bread, fresh or toasted
1 recipe vegan omelettes (see opposite page)

method

To make the sauce, combine the flour, yeast and olive oil in a small saucepan and mix until evenly combined and no lumps remain. Stir through the vegan milk, a little at a time, then place on the stove over medium heat. Bring to the boil while stirring, reduce the heat to low and continue to stir for another two minutes. Take off the heat while you prepare the rest of the meal. When ready to serve, adjust the seasonings with vinegar and salt, then briefly reheat until bubbling.

To make the greens with onions, remove the green leaves from the stalks and rip or chop into thin pieces. Wash and dry using a salad spinner and set aside. Heat the olive oil in a medium saucepan over medium-high heat, then sauté the onion and salt until fragrant and golden in places. Set aside until you wish to serve, when the rest of the dish is ready, quickly put the pan back on the heat and stir through the greens until wilted and brightly coloured. For an onion-free option, just use the oil and salt to cook the kale, or steam it instead.

Make the omelettes according to the directions on the opposite page. When the omelettes are ready, assemble the meal by placing a large slice of bread on each plate, topping with the omelettes. Reheat the sauce and cook the greens, then place on top of the omelettes and serve with plenty of cracked pepper.

Gluten-Free Option: Ensure that your bread and flour are gluten-free.

fast bean and tahini pasta sauce

Mildly flavoured with tahini this is a delicious creamy pasta sauce that can be made while the pasta is boiling.

Gluten-Free Option, Soy-Free Option,
Nightshade-Free, Onion- and Garlic-Free Option
No Specialty Ingredients, No Nuts
Under 45 Minutes
Kitchen time 5 minutes
Total time 15-20 minutes
Serves 2

ingredients

2 tablespoons tahini (preferably unhulled)
1 tablespoon mellow light miso, or 1 tablespoon nutritional yeast plus 1/2 teaspoon salt
1-3 cloves of garlic, optional
1 teaspoon agave or unrefined sugar
2 teaspoons apple cider vinegar
1 cup of water
1 1/2 cups cooked beans (eg. borlotti, pinto, cannellini, chickpeas)

method

While your pasta is boiling, combine all the ingredients in a blender. Blend until smooth. Drain the pasta and heat the sauce up over medium heat. Once the sauce is bubbling, add the pasta and stir through, until hot. Serve right away with a green salad.

bean bolognese

Another delicious and easy way to serve pasta that can be made while the pasta is boiling.

Gluten-Free Option, Soy-Free, Onion- and Garlic-Free Option
No Specialty Ingredients Option, No Nuts
Under 45 Minutes
Kitchen time 5 minutes
Total time 15-20 minutes
Serves 2

ingredients

water, for boiling
wholegrain pasta for 2 serves
optional onion and garlic, to sauté
1 - 1 1/2 cups prepared pasta sauce
1 - 1 1/2 cups cooked beans
red wine vinegar and salt, to taste
optional olives and/or nutritional yeast, to taste

method

Bring some water to the boil for the pasta.

If you can be bothered with an extra step for an extra tasty sauce, sauté some onion for a few minutes, until tender and fragrant, then add garlic and stir through for a few more seconds. Add the prepared pasta sauce and beans and bring to the boil. Reduce the heat and simmer while waiting for the pasta to cook, adjust seasonings to taste with red wine vinegar and salt, adding some olives and/or nutritional yeast for extra flavour if you wish. Serve the sauce on top of the pasta and sprinkle with extra nutritional yeast.

bok choy and chickpeas with miso and balsamic dressing

An exciting new way of cooking vegetables, with the incredibly delicious umami-rich flavours of miso and balsamic vinegar. If you wish to make this with cabbage or cauliflower instead of bok choy, you might want to increase the cooking time by another couple of minutes.

Gluten-Free Option,
Low Fat Option, Nightshade-Free
Onion- and Garlic-Free
No Specialty Ingredients, No Nuts
Under 45 minutes
Kitchen time 10 minutes
Serves 2

ingredients

Grains and water for cooking (quinoa will make this a very fast meal)
1 large bunch of bok choy, or other vegetables such as cabbage, cauliflower or broccoli
1 1/2- 2 1/4 cups cooked chickpeas
1/2 cup water
1 1/2 tablespoons mellow light miso
1 1/2 tablespoons balsamic vinegar
1 tablespoon olive oil or water

method

Cook the grains according to the directions on page 11.

While the grains are cooking, prepare your vegetables and chickpeas by rinsing and drying them in a salad spinner or colander. Chop the bok choy into pieces around 1 inch (3cm) long. Make the dressing by mixing the miso, balsamic vinegar and olive oil together in a small bowl.

When the grains have finished cooking, heat a heavy chef pan or stockpot over a high heat. When the pan is hot, add 2-4 teaspoons of olive oil and quickly throw in the bok choy stems first, and then the chickpeas and bok choy leaves. Put the lid on and cook for 2 minutes without stirring or lifting the lid.

Add half a cup of water to the pan and stir through. Put the lid back on and cook for another 2 minutes. Taste some of the bok choy to see if it's cooked enough and cook for a little longer if needed. Take off the heat and stir through the dressing. Serve right away on top of the grains.

Soy-free and gluten-free options: use a soy-free and gluten-free miso

17

spanish chard with beans, raisins, sunflower seeds and garlic

An incredibly tasty way to eat a lot of greens in one meal with a little sweetness from the raisins, crunch from the chard stems and umami flavours from the smoked paprika and miso.

I like to serve this with brown rice or other cooked wholegrains (use quinoa for a really fast meal), but bread or roasted veggies are also good choices.

Gluten-Free Option, Soy-Free Option
Nightshade-Free Option
No Nuts, Under 45 Minutes
Kitchen time 10 minutes
Serves 2

ingredients

1/2 cup water, for soaking raisins
4 tablespoons raisins or sultanas
4 tablespoons sunflower seeds
1 bunch swiss chard or silverbeet (around 500g/1.1lb)
1-2 tablespoons olive oil
3 large cloves of garlic, thinly sliced
1 1/2 cups cooked azduki, borlotti or pinto beans
1-2 teaspoons miso, tamari or coconut aminos
optional smoked paprika, to taste

method

Bring the water to the boil, take off the heat and soak the raisins in it while you prepare the rest of the dish.

Toast the sunflower seeds in a dry frying pan over medium heat, stirring frequently until golden. Set aside.

Cut the chard, including the stalks into one inch (2.5cm) pieces.

Heat the olive oil in a frying pan and sauté the garlic until golden. Add the chard and sauté for one minute. Stir through the beans until the chard is wilted and the beans are hot. Drain the raisins and add these, along with the sunflower seeds. Adjust the seasonings with miso and smoked paprika. Serve right away.

Soy-Free and Gluten-Free Options: If using miso, check that it is suitable

pasta alla carbonara

Creamy, comforting and full of umami flavour this is a hearty pasta meal that can be made in minimal time.

Gluten-Free Option,
Nightshade-Free
Under 45 MInutes
Total time 15-20 minutes
Serves 2

ingredients

water, for boiling
7oz-10oz (200g-300g) spaghetti or other wholegrain pasta

2/3 cup cashews
2/3 cup water

1 tablespoon olive oil
half a medium onion, diced

1 1/2 cups peas, fresh or frozen

2 teaspoons mellow light miso
1 teaspoon nutritional yeast (savoury yeast flakes)

method

Bring a pot of water to the boil, for cooking the pasta.

While waiting for the pot to boil, combine the cashews and water in a blender and leave to soak for a few minutes.

Sauté the onion in the olive oil until golden and fragrant.

When the pasta water is boiling, add the pasta. Cook according to the packet directions, adding the peas for the last two minutes of cooking. Drain.

Switch the blender on to make a creamy sauce from the cashews and water. Blend until smooth, then pour into the sauté pan with the onions and bring to the boil. Stir through the miso and nutritional yeast. Add the pasta and peas, stirring to cover them completely in the sauce. Serve right away.

Soy-free option: use a soy-free miso
Gluten-free option: Choose a gluten-free pasta and ensure your miso is gluten-free

pasta with broccoli and mushrooms in a creamy sauce

A simple and delicious pasta meal, full of mushroom flavours and crunchy just-cooked-enough broccoli.

ingredients

Gluten-Free Option, Soy-Free
Nightshade-Free
No Specialty Ingredients Option,
Under 45 Minutes
Total time 15-20 minutes
Serves 2

water, for boiling
200g-300g (7oz-10oz) wholegrain pasta

1/4 cup cashews
1 cup water
1 1/2 cups cooked cannellini beans, or other white beans
1/4 teaspoon unrefined sugar
1/2 - 1 teaspoon salt, to taste
1/2 teaspoon apple cider vinegar or lemon juice
optional 1 teaspoon nutritional yeast (savoury yeast flakes)
optional pinch of nutmeg
1/2 teaspoon balsamic vinegar or lemon juice
1 teaspoon cracked pepper, or to taste

1 medium onion, sliced into half or quarter moons
250g (8.8oz) fresh mushrooms, thinly sliced
1 medium head of broccoli, broken or cut into small florets around the same size

method

Bring a pot of water to the boil for the pasta.

While you're waiting for the water to boil, combine the cashews, water, cannellini beans, sugar, salt, cider vinegar, nutritional yeast and nutmeg in a blender. Leave to sit for a few minutes, for the cashews to soak.

Chop up the onion, mushrooms and broccoli.

Sauté the onion in plenty of olive oil over medium-high heat until tender and fragrant, around five minutes. Stir through the mushrooms and continue to cook, stirring every now and again for another 3 minutes or so, until the mushrooms are soft and coloured.

When the pasta water is boiling, add the pasta. Cook according to packet directions, adding the broccoli and putting the lid on for the last two minutes of pasta cooking time. Drain.

Blend the sauce ingredients in the blender until smooth and pour into the frying pan with the onion and mushrooms. Bring to the boil, reduce the heat and simmer for a minute or two, until thickened. Add the balsamic vinegar and cracked pepper, along with the drained pasta and broccoli.

Gluten-free option: Choose a gluten-free pasta

grains, beans and veggies

A simple and nourishing meal that can be made really quickly from whatever is on hand. I like to use quinoa, or a mix of quinoa and amaranth for the grain. Freshly cooked beans are great in this, but canned ones will be fine.

Gluten-Free Option, Soy-Free Option
Nightshade-Free Option,
Onion- and Garlic-Free Option
Low Fat Option
No Specialty Ingredients Option
No Nuts Option, Under 45 Minutes

ingredients

Per one serve:
1/2 cup grain (eg. quinoa, amaranth, brown rice)
a tiny pinch of salt
water, for cooking the grain (the amount depends which grain you're using. Use 1 cup for quinoa or amaranth)
2/3 cup to 1 cup of cooked beans
raw or cooked vegetables of your choice

method

Cook the grains according to the directions on page 11.

Prepare the sauce and vegetables while the grains are cooking.

Place the grains on plates, top with the cooked beans, vegetables and any extra toppings such as pickled veggies, then drizzle with the sauce.

quinoa, lentils, red cabbage, mesclun mix, pickled gherkin slices and spring onions, drizzled with tahini sauce (page 96)

miso and balsamic sauce

makes 2 serves

optional 2-4 small cloves of garlic, skin removed
a pinch of salt
4 1/2 tablespoons olive oil (or replace some of this with water for a lower fat option)
1 1/2 tablepoons mellow light miso
1 1/2 tablespoons balsamic vinegar

Crush the garlic in a mortar and pestle with the salt until smooth. Add the rest of the ingredients and stir. Place in a larger bowl and whisk with a fork until blended.

quinoa and amaranth, topped with chickpeas, grilled (broiled) tomatoes, salad greens and red cabbage, and served with a miso, balsamic and garlic sauce.

21

pumpkin and pesto salad

This meal salad is delicious served hot or cold, great for picnics, pot lucks and lunch boxes. It will keep for up to a week in the fridge. Best served with a green salad on the side.

Gluten-Free,   Low Fat Option,
Nightshade-Free, Onion- and Garlic-Free Option
No Specialty Ingredients
No Nuts Option, Under 45 Minutes
Kitchen time 15 minutes
Total time 45 minutes
Serves 4

ingredients

1.55lb (700g) butternut pumpkin (or other winter squash/pumpkin)
1 1/2 cups quinoa or amaranth, or a mixture
2 3/4 cups cold water
4.4oz (125g) spinach, kale or swiss chard (silverbeet)
1 recipe pesto from this page, either basil or arugula
3 cups cooked chickpeas

method

Preheat the oven to 350f (175c). Chop the pumpkin into around 8 pieces, leaving the skin on. Place on a lined baking sheet, skin side down.

Bake for around 30 minutes, or until soft. Allow to cool before removing the skin and slicing. Chop into 1/2" (2cm) cubes.

Rinse and drain the grains several times, then place in a medium-sized saucepan with the water. Bring to the boil over medium-high heat, then turn the heat down to a simmer and cook for 15 minutes with the lid on. Turn off the heat, place the spinach on top of the grains, put the lid back on and allow to stand for 10 minutes.

Prepare the pesto according to the directions on this page.

To assemble:
Put the cooked grains, spinach and chickpeas in a large mixing bowl. Stir through the pesto. Place on on individual plates and top with the pumpkin.

Arugula Pesto (nut-free)
1/4 Cup pumpkin seeds, preferably toasted
1 tablespoon mellow light miso or nutritional yeast
a pinch of salt (add an extra pinch if using nutritional yeast)
1 1/2 packed cups arugula (rocket)
3 tablespoons olive oil
2 tablespoons water

Process the pumpkin seeds in a food processor until they are in small, fairly even pieces. Add the miso, arugula, olive oil and water. Process until evenly mixed through.

Basil Pesto
1/4 cup cashews
2 teaspoons nutritional yeast
1 clove of garlic (optional)
1/2 teaspoon salt
1/2 teaspoon cracked pepper
1.75oz (50g) fresh basil
3 tablespoons olive oil or water

In a food processor combine the cashews, nutritional yeast, garlic, salt and pepper. Process until the cashews are in small, fairly even pieces. Add the basil and olive oil, process until evenly mixed through.

23

taco beans in crisp lettuce

This can be made as a raw meal, using sprouted beans, or with cooked beans served hot or cold. Either way, this makes a delicious, fast and healthy meal.

Gluten-Free Option, Soy-Free Option,
Low Fat, No Nuts
No Specialty Ingredients, Under 45 Minutes
Kitchen time 5-10 minutes
Serves 2

ingredients

For raw beans:
1/2 tablespoon lemon juice
1 tablespoon miso, tamari or coconut aminos
1 teaspoon ground cumin
a pinch of cayenne pepper
half a small red onion, finely diced
2 1/2 cups sprouted beans (azduki, mung beans,
chickpeas or lentils)
optional pinch of salt, to taste

For cooked beans:
1/2 tablespoon lemon juice
1 tablespoon miso, tamari or coconut aminos
1 teaspoon ground cumin
a pinch of cayenne pepper
half a small red onion, finely diced
2 cups cooked beans (adzuki, black, pinto, kidney or
brown lentils)
optional pinch of salt, to taste

To serve:
1 large head of cos (romaine) or iceberg
lettuce
1-2 cups cooked rice, or grated raw vegetables
Optional extra toppings (eg. avocado, tomatoes, onion,
lime juice, prepared salsa)

method

To prepare the raw bean mixture: Combine all ingredients except for the beans in a mixing bowl, breaking up the pieces of onion. Stir through the beans and serve.

To prepare the cooked bean mixture: Combine the lemon juice, miso, cumin, cayenne pepper and red onion in a mixing bowl, breaking up the pieces of onion. For hot beans, place the beans in a saucepan with a tiny bit of water and bring to the boil with the lid on over medium heat. Remove the lid, stir and cook until the water has evaporated, then add to the bowl with the other ingredients.

potato and chickpea salad

This hearty salad is perfect for sharing at a picnic, potluck or barbecue. It can be served straight away at room temperature, or can be kept in the fridge for a few days. It has more protein than a typical potato salad, thanks to the addition of chickpeas, so it only needs a green salad to complete it as a meal for two.

Gluten-Free Option,
No Specialty Ingredients Option
Under 45 Minutes
Kitchen time 5-10 minutes
Cooking time 20 minutes
Serves 4 as a side dish, or 2 as a main

ingredients

1.5lbs (700g) potatoes (9 small-medium ones)
a handful of chopped fresh chives
half a handful of chopped fresh parsley
optional 1 tablespoon mellow light miso*
10 tablespoons (2/3 cup) cashew mayonnaise
1 1/2 cups cooked chickpeas

cashew mayonnaise

1 cup raw cashews
1 cup water
1 tablespoon apple cider vinegar
1/4 cup vegan milk
1/4 - 1/2 cup olive oil
salt and pepper to taste (I use around half a teaspoon of each)

In a blender, soak the cashews in the water and vinegar for at least a couple of minutes, or up to 24 hours. Blend until smooth, then blend in the vegan milk. Slowly drizzle in the olive oil while blending. Add salt and pepper to taste. This will keep in the fridge for up to a week.

method

Bring a pot of water to the boil over medium-high heat. Scrub any dirt off the potatoes and chop them into bite-sized pieces. When the water is boiling, add the potatoes. Cook with the lid on for 20 minutes, reducing the heat to medium-low if it's boiling over. Drain and rinse with cold water until they cool down.

In large mixing bowl combine the chives, parsley, miso and mayonnaise, stirring until the miso is thoroughly mixed in. Stir through the chickpeas to coat in the dressing, then mix in the potato. Eat right away, or refrigerate for up to five days.

Soy-free and gluten-free options: Use a soy-free and gluten-free miso

raw summer rolls with toasted sesame seeds and cashews

These are inspired by delicious tasting rice paper rolls. For this recipe I've gotten rid of all the white rice noodles and replaced them with crisp raw vegetables and sprouts to form a refreshing and satisfying meal with plenty of protein. These are best served as make-your-own wraps, with separate dishes for the seeds, filling, leaves and sauce.

Gluten-Free Option, Soy-Free Option,
No Specialty Ingredients Option
Under 45 Minutes
Total time 15-20 minutes
Serves 4

ingredients

For the seeds:
3 tablespoons sesame seeds
4 tablespoons cashews

For the filling:
1 red capsicum (red pepper)
half a small cabbage (500g/1.1lb), cored
1 medium carrot
3 cups mung bean sprouts
2 pinches of salt, or to taste

24 large lettuce or cabbage leaves

For the optional sauce:
2 tablespoons mellow light miso*
1/3 cup water
1 tablespoon apple juice concentrate or agave
1 tablespoon apple cider vinegar
1 tablespoon lime or lemon juice
1 clove garlic, very finely chopped
1-3 pinches of cayenne pepper, to taste

method

Toast the seeds and cashews in a small dry saucepan over medium-high heat, stirring often until lightly toasted. Roughly grind in the food processor or chop by hand.

Using the grating attachment of a food processor, or a hand grater and knife, finely shred the capsicum, cabbage and carrot. Add to a large bowl and stir through the mung bean sprouts and salt, to taste.

To make the sauce, combine all the ingredients in a small bowl and whisk to combine.

*Soy-free and gluten-free options: Use a soy-free and gluten-free miso

caesar salad with crispy chickpea and cauliflower fritters

A meal salad to be enjoyed even by those who appreciate neither cauliflower or salad. The fresh crunch of lettuce balances out the richness of the fritters, complimented by an incredibly delicious creamy caesar salad dressing. The dressing makes enough for four serves and will keep in the fridge for up to a week.

Gluten-Free Option,
Onion- and Garlic-Free Option
Under 45 Minutes
Kitchen time 15 minutes
Total time 15 minutes
Serves 2

ingredients

For the dressing:
3/4 cup cashews
3/4 cup water
1 teaspoon vegan worcestershire sauce
3 teaspoons dijon mustard
2 teaspoons mellow light miso, or nutritional yeast plus salt, to taste
1 clove garlic, optional
2 tablespoons lemon juice or apple cider vinegar
2 tablespoons olive oil

For the fritters:
1/2 a medium cauliflower (17oz/500g, 1 lightly heaped dinner plate after chopping)
1 cup chickpea flour
2/3 cup water
1 tablespoon miso, or nutritional yeast plus 1 teaspoon salt
optional 2 cloves garlic, finely chopped or crushed

6.3oz (180g) romaine (cos) lettuce leaves
optional 2 tablespoons capers

method

Combine all the dressing ingredients except for the olive oil in the blender and leave to soak for a couple of minutes, or up to 8 hours. Blend until creamy, then drizzle in the olive oil while the blender is going, blending for a further 30 seconds after the oil is added.

Cut the cauliflower florets into thin slices, around 1/4" (1/2cm) thick.

In a mixing bowl break up any lumps in the chickpea flour, then add the water to form a thick batter. Stir through the miso and garlic until evenly mixed. Stir through the cauliflower pieces, to coat.

Cover the base of a large pan with olive oil roughly 1/3" (3/4cm) deep. Heat the oil over medium-high heat, keeping an eye out to watch until it's hot. To test the heat, add a piece of the coated cauliflower, the oil should fizz up around the cauliflower right away. Fry the cauliflower in batches until golden-brown, flipping the pieces over halfway through frying. It takes three batches in a 9.5" (24cm) chef pan. Alternatively the fritters can be baked on a greased baking sheet at 350f (175c) for 20-30 minutes.

While the cauliflower is frying, assemble a bed of lettuce leaves on each plate. Drizzle with the dressing. Top with the cauliflower fritters and sprinkle with capers and extra dressing if you wish.

marinated kale salad
with apples, beans, sunflower seeds and cranberries

A delicious and filling salad with plenty of protein. Eat on its own, or serve with bread, roasted veggies or cooked grains for a complete meal. While most salad greens are best coated in dressing right before serving, kale benefits from being marinated for longer, to tenderise the leaves. This salad can be served right away or kept in the fridge for later.

Gluten-Free, Soy-Free
Nightshade-Free
Onion- and Garlic-Free
No Nuts, Under 45 Minutes
Kitchen time 10 minutes
Serves 2

ingredients
1 small bunch of kale (8 loose cups after the stems are ripped off)
3 tablespoons olive oil
1 tablespoon red wine vinegar
1 tablespoon dijon mustard
a pinch of salt
1/3 cup sunflower seeds
1 small apple
1/2 cup dried cranberries
1 1/2 cups cooked adzuki, borlotti, pinto, or black eye beans

method
Rip the stems off the kale and tear or chop the leaves into smaller pieces. In a large mixing bowl combine the olive oil, vinegar, mustard and salt and whisk with a fork until smooth. Coat all the kale in this dressing and set aside while the other ingredients are prepared.

Toast the sunflower seeds in a dry pan over medium heat, shaking the pan often, until mostly golden. Pour onto a small plate and set aside.

Cut the apple in half, remove the seeds and the tough core and cut into thin slices. Mix this in with the kale and dressing.

Add the toasted sunflower seeds, cranberries and beans to the kale and mix to combine.

bean and mushroom stroganoff

The traditional Russian stew made into a healthy and hearty high protein vegan meal. This has sour flavours from the vegan sour cream, a slight spiciness from mustard seeds and pepper along with a lot of satisfying umami flavours from the mushrooms and tomato purée. Great served with potatoes, cooked grains, bread or pasta.

Gluten-Free Option, Soy-Free Option
No Specialty Ingredients
No Nuts Option, Under 45 Minutes
Kitchen time 15-20 minutes
Total time 30-40 minutes
Serves 8

ingredients

3 tablespoons yellow mustard seeds

1-2 tablespoons olive oil

2 medium-large onions, in quarter moons

9 oz (250g) mushrooms, sliced

2 tablespoons flour (barley, wheat, spelt or gluten-free)

2 1/2 cups water (preferably cooking water from cooking the beans)

1 1/2 cups tomato purée or diced tomatoes

7 1/2 cups cooked borlotti or pinto beans

1 1/2 cups vegan sour cream (eg. cashew sour cream, page 96) or vegan buttermilk*

optional chopped fresh parsley, to serve

method

Heat the mustard seeds over medium-high heat in a dry stockpot or large saucepan until they begin to pop. Add the oil and onions and sauté for around 5 minutes, until the onions are tender and fragrant. Add the mushrooms and sauté for two more minutes.

Stir through the flour, then stir through the water and tomato purée. Add the beans and bring to the boil. Reduce the heat, remove the lid and simmer over a low heat for at least ten minutes. Stir through the vegan sour cream, sprinkle with parsley and serve.

Serving options: This can be made into a stroganoff shepherds pie by pouring the stew into baking dishes, topping it with mashed potato and baking until the potato is crispy on top.

*To make vegan buttermilk, mix 1 1/2 cups almond, cashew, hazelnut or sunflower seed milk with 1 1/2 tablespoons vinegar and allow to sit and curdle for five minutes). For a soy-free cashew sour cream recipe, see page 96.

black bean soup

A hearty and warming soup with just the right amount of spice. The smoked paprika gives it a really special smokey taste, but this soup will taste just as great using regular paprika instead.

Gluten-Free Option,
No Specialty Ingredients Option
Low Fat, No Nuts
Kitchen time: 10 minutes
Soaking time: 8-16 hours
Cooking time: 1 hour
Serves 4

ingredients

1.1lb/500g (2 2/3 cups) dry black beans
water, for soaking
2 medium onions, diced
3 big cloves of garlic, finely chopped
4 teaspoons ground cumin
6 cups water
2 teaspoons smoked paprika (regular paprika will also work, if you don't have the smoked kind)
1/4 - 1 teaspoon cayenne pepper, to taste
salt, to taste
1 teaspoon red wine vinegar, or apple cider vinegar, lemon juice or lime juice
optional tablespoon miso, tamari or coconut aminos

method

Rinse the black beans and soak in water for 8-16 hours.

Sauté the onions in a stockpot or large saucepan until tender and fragrant, around five minutes. Stir through the garlic for a minute longer, then stir through the cumin for 30 seconds and pour in 6 cups of water.

Rinse and drain the soaked beans and add these to the pot. Bring to the boil. Boil rapidly for one or two minutes, reduce the heat and simmer with the lid on until the beans are tender, around an hour.

Add the paprika, cayenne pepper, salt, vinegar and miso.

Serve with bread or corn chips, and some crisp lettuce.

Gluten-free and soy-free options: omit the optional miso, or check the ingredients to make sure it is suitable.

31

beetroot and adzuki bean (or lentil) curry

Subtly spiced so that the natural flavours of the beetroot can shine, this is a great use of the often-neglected ingredients of adzuki beans and beetroot.

Gluten-Free,
No Specialty Ingredients
Low Fat, Nightshade-Free Option
Onion- and Garlic-Free, No Nuts
Kitchen time 10 minutes
Total time 20 minutes, plus beetroot cooking time
Serves 6

ingredients

2 teaspoons cumin seeds
2 1/2 teaspoons mustard seeds (brown or yellow)
1-2 tablespoons coconut oil, or other cooking oil
3 bay leaves or curry leaves
1 teaspoon turmeric
6 cups peeled and roughly chopped cooked beetroot*
1/2 cup water
4 1/2 cups cooked azduki beans or brown lentils
1 tablespoon lemon juice or apple cider vinegar
salt, to taste
optional pinch of cayenne pepper, to taste

method

In a dry stockpot or large saucepan heat the cumin seeds and mustard seeds over a medium heat until they begin to make popping sounds, shaking the pan every so often.   Pour in the oil, then quickly stir through the bay leaves and turmeric for 30 seconds.

Stir through the beetroot, then add the water and beans. Bring to the boil, reduce the heat and simmer for at least five minutes. Stir through the lemon juice and add salt and cayenne pepper, to taste.

*To prepare the beetroots for this recipe, wash them (don't peel) and place in a saucepan with enough water to cover. Bring to the boil with the lid on, reduce the heat and gently simmer with the lid on until tender and the skins can easily be removed by rubbing - around 40 minutes for small ones, 1-2 hours for large. Remove from the heat, drain, and place back in the saucepan with enough cold water to cover for around 10 minutes, until they are cold enough to handle. Peel the skins off using your hands (if they are properly cooked, this will be easy), then roughly chop into bite-sized pieces. Any leftover cooked beetroots make a great addition to salads and sandwiches, or as a cold sliced vegetable on the side of a meal.

fast stovetop 'baked' beans

A welcome change from the usual style of baked beans, these are excellent served with baked potatoes or oven chips. The miso adds depth to the flavour of this dish, which no one would guess was made in a few minutes on the stove.

Gluten-Free Option,
No Specialty Ingredients
Low Fat, Onion- and Garlic-Free Option
No Nuts, Under 45 Minutes
Kitchen time 5 minutes
Total time 7 minutes
Serves 2

ingredients

3/4 cup tomato purée (or diced tomatoes)
1 teaspoon apple juice concentrate, agave or sugar
2 teaspoons apple cider vinegar
1-2 cloves of garlic, finely chopped (optional)
a pinch or two of cayenne pepper
optional teaspoon of olive oil
1 1/2 - 2 1/4 cups cooked beans (cannellini, navy, butter, lima, borlotti, pinto or black eye beans will work best)
2 teaspoons miso (preferably a mellow light variety)

method

Place all the ingredients except for the miso in a small saucepan over medium-high heat and bring to the boil. Reduce the heat and simmer for at least two minutes, adding a little water if needed. Mix through the miso and serve.

Gluten-free option: use a gluten-free miso
Soy-free option: use a soy-free miso

sunchoke crisps on cannellini bean and sunchoke purée with arugula pesto

An unusual and delicious combination of textures and flavours. Proof that it's possible to make high protein and nutritious meals that look impressive on a plate.

Gluten-Free Option, Soy-Free Option,
Nightshade-Free, Onion- and Garlic-Free
No Nuts, Under 45 Minutes
Kitchen time 20 minutes
Total time 30 minutes
Serves 2

ingredients

For the pesto:
1/4 Cup pumpkin seeds, preferably toasted
1 tablespoon mellow light miso or nutritional yeast
a pinch of salt (add an extra pinch of using nutritional yeast)
1 1/2 packed cups arugula (rocket)
3 tablespoons olive oil
2 tablespoons water

For the purée:
11oz (325g) sunchokes (jerusalem artichokes)
1 1/2 cups cooked cannellini beans, or other white bean
salt, to taste

For the crisps:
11oz (325g) sunchokes (jerusalem artichokes)
salt, to taste

method

Make the pesto by placing the pumpkin seeds, miso, salt and arugula in a food processor. Process into small pieces, then add the olive oil and water. Process more to form a thick sauce.

Scrub the dirt off all the sunchokes. Place the ones for the purée in a saucepan with cold water, to cover. Bring to the boil. Boil for 15 minutes, or until fork-tender. Drain and purée in the food processor or mash with the cannellini beans, adding some salt, to taste. Place in a small saucepan and bring to the boil over medium heat, stir, then reduce the heat to low until you're ready to serve the dish.

Using the slicing side of a grater, or the mandoline attachment for a food processor (or just using a knife) make thin slices with the remaining sunchokes, for frying.

Coat the base of a chef pan or large saucepan with 1/2" (1cm) of olive oil (or other cooking oil). Heat the oil over medium-high heat until hot enough to fry (to test, place a slice of sunchoke in the oil, when it is lightly golden, the oil is ready to fry the rest of the sunchokes). Fry in batches until lightly golden, around 1-2 minutes. It takes three batches in a 10" (24cm) chef pan. Drain in a tea towel over a colander and sprinkle with a little salt. The crisps will become darker after they've been removed from the oil.

To assemble, scatter plates with arugula leaves if you wish, place the purée in the centre of the dish, then top with the sunchoke crisps. Drizzle the pesto around the plate and on top of the purée.

potato and pea curry

The classic Indian restaurant curry - the way it should be. Some of the potatoes break down to form a thick gravy that's full of flavour but mildly spiced. If you want a really decadent restaurant-style curry, add the coconut or cashew cream and prepare to be impressed.

Gluten-Free,
No Specialty Ingredients, Low Fat
No Nuts, Under 45 Minutes
Kitchen time 15-20 minutes
Total time 45 minutes
Serves 8

ingredients

2.65lb (1.2kg) potatoes (16 small-medium ones, around 9 cups after chopping)
optional 3-4 tablespoons brown mustard seeds
2 onions, sliced into in half moons
4 cloves garlic, finely chopped
1 tablespoon finely chopped fresh ginger, or 1 teaspoon dry
2 teaspoons turmeric
1 teaspoon cumin
2 teaspoons garam masala
3-4 cups water
salt and cayenne pepper, to taste
optional 1/2 cup coconut cream or cashew cream
5-6 cups fresh or frozen peas (28oz/800g)

method

Bring half a stockpot or large saucepan of water to the boil. Add the potatoes and boil for 20 minutes, until fork-tender.

Prepare the other ingredients, along with some rice while the potatoes boil.

When the potatoes have boiled, drain them and dry the stockpot. Chop all the potatoes except for one into bite-sized pieces. Chop the remaining potato into tiny pieces so it will dissolve and thicken the sauce.

Put the dry stockpot back on the heat with the mustard seeds, shaking the pot every now and then, until they start to pop. Add a tablespoon or two of cooking oil, along with the onion. Stir this continuously until the onion is tender and fragrant, about 5 minutes. Stir through the garlic and fresh ginger, if using, for 30 seconds, then add the spices. Stir for another minute, then add the water and the potatoes.

Bring to the boil, smashing up some potatoes to thicken the sauce. Adjust the seasonings with salt and cayenne pepper, adding the optional coconut cream or cashew cream. Bring to the boil and check to make sure that the potatoes are cooked to perfection. Stir through the peas, bring to the boil again and cook for 5 more minutes. Serve with rice, crisp raw vegetables and maybe some pappadams.

thai green curry

A spicy and fragrant Thai curry that takes minimal kitchen time once the homemade curry paste is on hand. Excellent served with rice or noodles and some crisp raw vegetables.

Gluten-Free, Soy-Free
No Specialty Ingredients
No Nuts, Under 45 Minutes
Kitchen time 5-10 minutes
Total time 25-30 minutes
Serves 2

ingredients

4 tablespoons homemade green curry paste
2 cups homemade coconut milk (or 1 14oz (400g) tin, plus 1/2 cup water)
2-3 cups diced vegetables (eg. potato, sweet potato, carrot, pumpkin, cauliflower)
1 1/2 cups cooked chickpeas, or two servings of fried soy-free 'tofu'
miso, salt, lemon or lime juice, to taste

---

thai green curry paste

makes enough for 3 curries (6 serves)
kitchen time 20 minutes
5 large fresh green chilies
4 cloves of garlic
zest of 1 1/2 lemons or limes
2-4 spring onions (green onions)
1 cup cilantro (coriander leaves)
an inch-sized piece of fresh ginger
2 teaspoons coriander seeds
1/2 teaspoon salt
3 tablespoons cooking oil

Combine all ingredients in a food processor and process until evenly and finely chopped, or process a little bit at a time in a pestle and mortar. Use right away, or cover and store in the fridge for up to a month, or freeze for a few months.

method

Place the curry paste in a saucepan over medium-high heat and wait for it to bubble. Stir for a minute, then add the coconut milk. Chop up the vegetables and add these to the saucepan. Bring to the boil, reduce heat and simmer for around 20 minutes, or until the vegetables are tender.

Stir through the chickpeas and taste, adding some miso or salt and some lemon or lime juice if you wish.

pilau

An Indian rice dish made into a quick and easy meal. While the total time for this is 35-45 minutes, the rice and raisins can be cooked hours or days in advance, so that the rest of the dish comes together very quickly.

Gluten-Free,
No Specialty Ingredients
Nightshade-Free, Under 45 Minutes
Kitchen time 10 minutes
Total time 45 minutes
Serves 2

ingredients

1 1/4 cups brown rice
1/3 cup raisins or sultanas
2 1/2 cups water
1/4 cup cashews
1 small onion, finely chopped
1/2 teaspoon turmeric
1/4 teaspoon cinnamon
1/4 teaspoon cardamon (optional)
1 teaspoon garam masala
1 1/2 - 2 cups fresh or frozen peas
salt, to taste

method

Rinse the rice and drain, then place in a small saucepan with the raisins and water, bring to the boil. Reduce the heat and simmer, covered, for 25-30 minutes, then take off the heat, leave for 5-10 minutes.

In a frying pan, sauté the cashews in a little cooking oil over medium heat until lightly toasted. Remove the cashews from the pan, then add the onion and sauté until golden and fragrant. Stir through the spices for 30 seconds, then add the peas, cashews, rice and raisins and continue to cook, stirring often for another two minutes, or until the peas are cooked and the rice is hot.

pumpkin and red lentil soup

A simple and satisfying meal to be served with bread and salad. This comforting soup can be served as it is, or made spicier with some minced chili stirred through, or some spices such as cumin and sumac sprinkled over the top. This recipe easily doubles or triples, and stores well in the fridge or freezer.

Gluten-Free, Soy-Free
No Specialty Ingredients
Low Fat, Nightshade-Free
No Nuts, Under 45 Minutes
Kitchen time 10-15 minutes
Cooking time 15 minutes
Serves 2

ingredients

1 small onion, diced
2 cloves garlic, roughly chopped
1 small butternut pumpkin (1.1lb/500g) peeled and roughly chopped
1/2 cup dry red split lentils
2 cups water
1/2 - 1 teaspoon salt, or to taste
1 teaspoon apple cider vinegar, or to taste
cracked pepper, to serve

method

Sauté the onion over medium high heat until tender and fragrant. Add the garlic and stir for a few more seconds, then add the pumpkin and continue to stir for 30 seconds (if you're in a rush you can add the lentils and water before the pumpkin, and chop the pumpkin while it is brought to the boil). Add the water and lentils and bring to the boil. Reduce the heat and simmer for 15 minutes, or until the lentils are dissolved and the pumpkin is soft. Use an immersion blender to purée the soup, or transfer it in batches to a blender, or simply mash up the pumpkin.

spicy carrot and chickpea tagine

A Moroccan-style stew fragrant with cinnamon. Very fast to make and satisfying to eat. I like to serve this with quinoa cooked with currants.

Gluten-Free,
No Specialty Ingredients, Low Fat
No Nuts, Under 45 Minutes
Kitchen time 10 minutes
Total time 20-25 minutes
Serves 4

ingredients

1 onion, finely chopped
3-4 cloves of garlic, finely chopped
2 teaspoons turmeric
1-2 teaspoons cumin seeds
1 teaspoon cinnamon
1/2 teaspoon cayenne pepper
1/2 teaspoon ground black pepper
1 tablespoon agave, or unrefined sugar
3-4 medium carrots, sliced into thick circles
3 cups cooked chickpeas
salt, to taste
optional fresh coriander leaves (cilantro), to serve
optional vegan yoghurt or cashew cream, to serve

method

Sauté the onion in some olive oil over a medium-high heat for around 5 minutes, until tender and fragrant. Stir through the garlic for another 30 seconds, then stir through the turmeric and cumin for 30-60 seconds. Add the cinnamon, cayenne, pepper, agave and carrots. Pour in enough water to cover the base of the pan, bring to the boil, reduce the heat and simmer with the lid on for 15 minutes.

Add the chickpeas, and some more water if needed. Bring to the boil, reduce heat and cook with the lid on for 5-10 more minutes, until the carrots are tender and the chickpeas are heated through.

Add salt, to taste and serve with cooked grains or bread, sprinkled with coriander leaves if you wish.

gigantes in olive and tomato sauce

A hearty Greek-inspired stew that can be made in minimal time. Fans of olives, even if they don't usually enjoy Greek food, will especially appreciate this meal. I like to serve this with quinoa.

Gluten-Free, Soy-Free
No Specialty Ingredients
No Nuts, Under 45 Minutes
Kitchen time 10 minutes
Total time 20 minutes
Serves 6

ingredients

1 large onion, finely diced
5-8 cloves of garlic, roughly chopped
1/3 cup water
1.5lb (700g) tomato purée or diced tomatoes
1 1/4 cups dark olives (preferably kalamata), pitted and roughly chopped
1 tablespoon red wine vinegar
1/2 teaspoon salt, or to taste
1 teaspoon dried oregano
1/4 teaspoon nutmeg
4 1/2 cups cooked lima beans (butter beans)

method

Heat some olive oil in a stockpot or large saucepan. Add the onion and sauté until tender and fragrant, around five minutes. Add the garlic and stir for a minute longer before adding the water, tomato purée, olives, vinegar, salt, oregano and nutmeg. Bring to the boil.

Gently stir through the beans and bring back to the boil. Reduce the heat and simmer with the lid off for at least five minutes.

Serve with fresh bread or a grain, along with some salad.

pumpkin and chickpea masala

Pumpkin and chickpeas cooked in a fragrant mix of spices.

ingredients

2 teaspoons coriander seeds, crushed in a pestle and mortar

2 teaspoons cumin seeds

1 teaspoon fennel seeds

1 teaspoon turmeric

1 teaspoon garam masala

2-3 medium onions, diced

optional 2 teaspoons fresh ginger, finely chopped

2kg (4.4lbs) butternut or other pumpkin (10 cups after slicing), cut into bite-sized pieces (not too small)

4 cups water

6 cups cooked chickpeas

1 tablespoon apple cider vinegar

2 teaspoons rapadura or other unrefined sugar

1 teaspoon salt, or to taste

optional 1/2 teaspoon cayenne pepper, or to taste

Gluten-Free,
No Specialty Ingredients
Low Fat, Nightshade-Free Option
No Nuts, Under 45 Minutes
Kitchen time 25 minutes
Total time 45-55 minutes
Serves 8-10

method

Prepare and measure out the spices, onions, ginger and pumpkin.

Sauté the onion over medium-high heat until tender and fragrant, around 5-10 minutes. Add the ginger, coriander, cumin and fennel seeds and continue to stir for another 30 seconds. Stir through the turmeric and garam masala for another 30 seconds, then add the pumpkin and water, stirring to combine. Add the chickpeas, apple cider vinegar and sugar and stir through. Bring to the boil, reduce the heat and simmer until the pumpkin is tender, around 20-30 minutes. Season with salt and cayenne pepper.

Nighshade-Free Option: Omit the cayenne pepper

soy-free tofu

soy-free tofu

Here is my basic recipe for soy-free tofu, it can be used in any of the recipes in this chapter, and also can take the place of soy tofu in many other dishes. It's not the same as soy tofu - it doesn't have the same texture or taste, but it is a protein-rich medium for all kinds of delicious sauces (like chermoula, pictured opposite), or to be fried up and used in a variety of recipes.

Burmese tofu has been traditionally made with chickpea flour for a long time, but it typically involves a lot of prep time and tricky steps, and while this would reduce the phytic acid in the tofu, it makes the process a lot slower. With my recipe the tofu can be ready to use in under 45 minutes. If you're good with planning ahead and want to make the tofu as nutritious as possible then the batter can definitely be soaked for 8 hours or more before heating it up, otherwise enjoy this cheap, fast and tasty homemade alternative to tofu.

Gluten-Free,
Low Fat, Nightshade-Free
Onion- and Garlic-Free
No Nuts, Under 45 Minutes
Kitchen time 10 minutes
Total time 40 minutes
Serves 4-6

ingredients
2 1/2 cups chickpea flour (besan)
1 teaspoon salt
4 cups cold water

method
Line or grease a 20x30cm (8x12") pan.

In a heavy-bottomed chef's pan, frying pan or saucepan place the chickpea flour and salt, and squash out any lumps. Add water a little at a time, making sure that no lumps form.

Turn on the heat to medium and stir continuously until very thick. I make this on an electric stove in a 9 1/2" (24cm) chef's pan and it takes around 7 minutes. If you're using a gas stove it will be quicker, if you're using a smaller saucepan it will take longer.

As soon as the mixture is very thick, quickly spread it into the prepared pan, pressing to form a flat, even surface (it will set very quickly). Refrigerate for at least half an hour before using as tofu.

To remove from the pan first slice into whatever shape you want them to be, and gently lift up. I find that lining the pan with a silicon baking mat or some baking paper makes it a lot easier to remove.

This will keep in the fridge for up to a week and can be used in all kinds of recipes that call for tofu.

baked soy-free tofu

Soy-free tofu does not need to be marinated before baking. To make baked tofu in either of these ways, simply mix all the ingredients together, cut the tofu into slices and place on a lined or greased baking sheet, with some sauce spread on all sides of the tofu. Bake for 20-30 minutes, flipping over for the last few minutes if you wish. For the chermoula-baked soy-free tofu (pictured opposite), see page 93.

Spicy Aussie BBQ (serves 2)
1 clove garlic, crushed or very finely chopped
a pinch of salt
1 tablespoon toasted sesame oil (or other cooking oil)
2 tablespoons tomato ketchup
1 tablespoon vegan worcestershire sauce
1 teaspoon agave, apple juice concentrate or unrefined sugar
1 teaspoon apple cider vinegar
optional 1 teaspoon blackstrap molasses
optional 1/2 teaspoon miso
1/2 teaspoon paprika
a pinch or two of cayenne pepper

Garlic and Thyme (serves 2)
4-5 cloves garlic, crushed in a mortar and pestle with 2 pinches of salt until paste-like
1/2 teaspoon dried thyme, or 2 teaspoons fresh
optional 1 teaspoon nutritional yeast (savoury yeast flakes)
5 teaspoons olive oil
1 teaspoon red wine vinegar

grain-free pad thai

Pad Thai is a tasty sweet and sour dish usually made from white rice noodles. I've used cabbage instead for a nutritious and low carb alternative, and it tastes incredible. When the cabbage is first stir-fried and then cooked in the Pad Thai sauce it transforms into a mixture of soft noodle-like pieces, and some crunchier pieces for more variety in texture. The total kitchen time for this recipe may seem lengthy, but all the chopping and sauce making can be done at an earlier time, to be cooked up later as a meal in less than 20 minutes.

Gluten-Free Option, Soy-free Option
Under 45 Minutes
Preparation time 20-30 minutes
Cooking time 15-20 minutes
Serves 2

ingredients

For the tofu:
2 servings of soy-free tofu, cut into small shapes
2 tablespoons wholegrain flour (any kind)
oil, for shallow frying

1.65lb (750g) green cabbage (3/4 of a medium-sized one), quartered and then cut into long 'noodle' shapes
4 spring onions (green onions), finely chopped

For the sauce:
zest of half a lime
juice of 1 1/2 limes
2 tablespoons unrefined sugar
1 tablespoon miso, tamari or coconut aminos
2 tablespoons water
half a large fresh red chili, finely chopped (or 2 teaspoons of minced chili from a jar, or cayenne pepper, to taste)

1/4 cup chopped up roasted peanuts
1 cup of mung bean sprouts

To serve:
optional handful or two of coriander leaves (cilantro)
half a lime, sliced into wedges
extra chopped peanuts

method

For the tofu, cut into small squares, rectangles or triangles and coat with the flour.

Prepare the rest of the ingredients to be ready for cooking and chop up some extra peanuts to sprinkle on top when serving. Mix the lime zest, lime juice, unrefined sugar, miso, water and chili in a small bowl to make the sauce.

Heat 0.2" (1/2cm) of cooking oil in a chef's pan or wok until hot. Add the coated tofu and fry on one side until golden, carefully flip each piece over and fry the other side until golden. Remove from the pan and set aside.

Drain all the oil except for one or two tablespoons. Place back on the heat and stir-fry the cabbage and spring onions until the cabbage is reduced in volume and smells nice. Add the prepared sauce and peanuts and continue to stir fry for another minute or two until some of the cabbage is soft, with some crunchier pieces still remaining. Take off the heat and stir through the mung bean sprouts and some of the tofu.

Serve in bowls or plates, garnishing with the rest of the tofu, some extra mung bean sprouts, peanuts, coriander leaves and lime wedges.

Soy-free option: use coconut aminos or a soy-free miso
Gluten-free option: make sure your flour and miso are gluten-free

chickpea chips

These are crunchy on the outside, soft on the inside, but they are not potato chips. Chickpea chips are much higher in protein, and lower in carbohydrates than potato chips, and they taste great. These chips give enough protein to a 'chip sandwich' to transform it from a carb-fest and into something resembling a balanced meal when served with a side salad.

Gluten-Free, Soy-Free
Nightshade-Free, Onion- and Garlic-Free
No Nuts, Under 45 Minutes
Total time 10 minutes
Serves 2

ingredients
2 servings soy-free tofu
oil, for frying

method
Slice the tofu into chip shapes, roughly 1cm (1/3") thick.

Pour 1-2cm (1/3-2/3") olive oil, or other cooking oil into a 24cm (10") pan. Heat over medium-high heat until hot enough to fry - when squiggly lines appear immediately in the oil after gently moving the pan. Test if it's hot enough by adding one chip to it, the oil should sizzle up around it right away. Place all the chips in the pan and leave to cook for around 4 minutes. Use a flipper to gently move the chips off the base of the pan, so that they are all floating in the oil. Stir them around to coat all sides of the oil and continue to fry until golden - around two more minutes.

When cooked, remove from the pan and drain in a colander lined with a tea towel. Serve with your favourite sauce. Because the chickpea tofu mixture has already been salted, there is no need to sprinkle the chips with salt.

salt and pepper tofu

Crispy cubes of pepper-flavoured 'tofu' served with a delicious sweet, salty and umami-rich sauté of leeks, garlic and ginger. For extra nutrition you could add some greens to the sauté.

Gluten-Free Option,
Nightshade-Free
No Nuts, Under 45 Minutes
Total time 10-15 minutes
Serves 2

ingredients

For the sauté:

3 small-medium leeks, finely chopped
2-3 cloves garlic, finely chopped
1 tablespoon finely chopped fresh ginger
1 tablespoon mellow light miso
1/2 teaspoon rapadura or other dark unrefined sugar
1/4 cup water

For the tofu:

2 serves soy-free tofu
water, for sprinkling
1 1/2 teaspoons cracked black pepper
1/2 teaspoon salt
4 tablespoons wholegrain flour (any kind)

method

Heat a little oil in a pan. Add the leeks, garlic and ginger and sauté until tender and fragrant, around 4 minutes. Stir through the miso and rapadura for 30 seconds, stir through the water, then set aside.

Cut the tofu into 1 inch cubes and place in a mixing bowl. Sprinkle with water, then sprinkle with the salt and pepper, tossing around to coat. Add the flour and continue to toss around until coated.

Cover the base of a large pan with 1/4" (1/2cm) oil and heat over a medium-high heat. When the oil is hot, add the tofu and fry on each side until golden.

Reheat the sauté and serve with rice or noodles - sesame and ginger rice (page 89) is a good choice.

Gluten-Free and Soy-Free Options:
Check that your miso and flour are gluten-free and soy-free

crispy tofu strips

Crispy, comforting and full of savoury flavour, these can also be made into smaller 'nuggets' if you prefer. Great served with oven chips, salad and tomato sauce.

Gluten-Free, Soy-Free
Nightshade-Free, Onion- and Garlic-Free
No Nuts, Under 45 Minutes
Total time 15 minutes
Serves 2

ingredients

3/4 cup chickpea flour
1 teaspoon dried sage
1 teaspoon dried thyme
1/2 teaspoon dried oregano
1/2 teaspoon dried rosemary
1/2 cup water
1 tablespoon miso, tamari or coconut aminos
2 teaspoons dijon mustard, optional
2/3 cup cornmeal
4 tablespoons nutritional yeast (savoury yeast flakes)
2 serves soy-free tofu
oil, for frying

method

Combine the chickpea flour and the herbs in a bowl. Add the water, a little at a time, to form a thick batter. Mix through the miso and mustard.

Mix the cornmeal with the nutritional yeast on a dinner plate.

Cut the tofu into 1/2" (1cm) thick strips, around 4" (10cm) long. Place each strip in the batter, to thickly coat it (but without too much excess batter), then roll in the cornmeal and nutritional yeast. Repeat for the remaining strips.

Coat the base of a 10" (24cm) frying pan with 1/4" (1/2cm) oil. Heat over a medium to medium-high heat. When the oil is hot enough to fry, gently place each tofu strip in the oil. Fry for around 4 minutes, until one side is golden-brown, then flip over and cook until the other side is golden, around 2 minutes.

laksa

A delicious and warming Malaysian meal with a spicy coconut-based broth, noodles, vegetables and fried soy-free tofu.

Gluten-Free Option, Soy-Free Option,
No Nuts, Under 45 Minutes
Total time 15 minutes
Serves 2

ingredients

For the soup:

4 tablespoons laksa paste (recipe below)

3 cups homemade coconut milk (or 1 1/2 cups canned, plus 1 1/2 cups extra water)

1 cup water

juice of one lime or lemon

1-2 tablespoons miso, tamari or coconut aminos

7 oz (200g) dry wholemeal spaghetti, or other wholegrain dry noodles

2 servings of soy-free tofu

1-2 tablespoons of flour, for coating

oil for shallow frying

1 medium carrot, chopped into matchsticks (or other fast-cooking vegetable)

1-2 cups broccoli florets (or other green vegetable)

1 cup kale, or other leafy green, ripped into small pieces

1 cup mung bean sprouts

2 handfuls of cilantro (coriander leaves)

homemade laksa paste

Kitchen time 12 minutes
Serves 4

1 small onion
1 clove of garlic
zest of one lime or lemon
1/2" (1cm) piece of fresh ginger
(or 1 1/2 teaspoons minced, or 1/4 teaspoon dried)
1-2 large red chilis, seeds removed
1/2 teaspoon turmeric
1 teaspoon coriander, ground
4 tablespoons olive oil

Place the onion, garlic, lime zest, ginger, chili, turmeric and coriander in a food processor. Blend until evenly chopped, then add the oil and continue to process until paste-like.

This makes around 8 tablespoons - enough for 4 serves. The leftover laksa paste will keep in the fridge for up to two weeks, or can be frozen for up to 6 months.

method

To make the soup: Place 4 tablespoons of the laksa paste in a saucepan over medium heat. When it begins to bubble, stir for a minute, then add the coconut milk and water. Bring to the boil, reduce the heat, and simmer.

Bring some water to the boil in another saucepan, then add the spaghetti. Cook according to the packet directions (mine takes 12 minutes) then drain and set aside.

While the spaghetti is cooking, wash and chop the vegetables and shallow fry the tofu.

To fry the tofu: If your stove only has two burners, then take the soup broth off the hotplate and place a saucepan with 1/4" (1/2cm) cooking oil on it over medium-high heat. Chop the tofu into cubes and toss them in some flour to coat. When the oil is hot, add the tofu and cook until one side is golden - around two minutes. Flip the cubes over to cook another side until golden, then gently stir fry for a minute longer. Drain and set aside. If you had to take the soup off the hotplate, put it back on now and leave it to simmer.

When everything else is ready, bring a saucepan with a tiny bit of water to the boil. Steam the carrot and broccoli for two minutes.

To serve: Place the noodles, carrot, broccoli, tofu, kale, sprouts and cilantro in two large noodle bowls. Add the lime juice and miso to the broth, adjusting the amounts to taste. Pour the broth into the bowl over the noodles and vegetables to serve.

49

satay tofu

Gluten-Free Option
Soy-Free Option
Under 45 Minutes
Kitchen Time: 20 minutes
Total time 30 minutes
Serves 2

Best served over brown rice or quinoa with leafy greens. To prepare the meal in this way first cook the grain according to the directions in this book. Prepare the sauce while the grain is cooking, then leave the sauce on the lowest heat setting while you cut the tofu and make the marinade. Cook the tofu, and lightly steam the greens while the tofu is cooking.

If you don't have the tofu already prepared, you can make this before you cook the grains and leave it to rest while the grains cook and the sauce is made. This will add to the kitchen time of the dish, but will still result in a meal on the table in less than 45 minutes.

ingredients

For the satay sauce:

a pinch of salt

1-2 cloves of garlic

1 medium onion

1 teaspoon-sized piece of fresh ginger

1 tablespoon peanuts, or peanut butter

zest of half a lemon

1 tablespoon coconut oil or other cooking oil

1/2 teaspoon garam masala

1/8 teaspoon turmeric

2 teaspoons lemon or lime juice

1 - 1 1/2 teaspoons finely minced red chili
(or cayenne pepper, to taste)

4 tablespoons peanut butter

1 1/4 cups homemade coconut milk (or use 3/4 cup canned with 1/2 cup water)

1 teaspoon unrefined sugar

miso or salt, to taste•

For the tofu:

2 servings soy-free tofu

optional 2 tablespoons mellow light miso

optional 1 tablespoon lime juice, lemon juice or vinegar

optional 1 tablespoon agave, or apple concentrate

optional 1 tablespoon olive oil

method

To make the sauce: Grind the salt, garlic, onion, ginger, peanuts and lemon zest in a mortar and pestle or food processor until ground into a paste with no large pieces remaining.

Heat the oil over a medium heat in a small saucepan and add the paste. Stir often until golden and fragrant, around 5 minutes. Add extra oil if you need to, to stop it sticking to the bottom of the pan.

Add the garam masala, turmeric, lime juice and chili to the saucepan and continue to fry while stirring for one minute. Stir through the peanut butter, coconut milk and sugar. Bring to the boil, reduce heat and simmer, stirring every now and then until the sauce has thickened, but can still be poured, around 5 minutes. Leave on the lowest heat setting while you prepare the rest of the dish. Add miso or salt, to taste.

To prepare the tofu: If using the marinade, whisk all the ingredients except for the tofu together in a mixing bowl. Cut the tofu into cubes or small shapes. Coat thoroughly in the marinade, if using. Put the cubes onto skewers if you wish.

Lightly brush or spray a grill pan or frying pan with oil. Heat it up over medium-high heat until hot, then place the tofu on it. When one side has finished cooking, rotate, and repeat until all other sides are charred in places.

*If you don't have miso, add a teaspoon or two of nutritional yeast for extra umami flavours

baked hash browns, for use as burger buns

Gluten-Free, Soy Free, **Low Fat**
Nightshade-Free Option
Onion- and Garlic-Free
No Nuts, Under 45 Minutes
Kitchen time 5-10 minutes
Cooking time 20-25 minutes
Serves 2

Preheat the oven to 175c (350f).

Grate 400g (14oz) of potatoes or sweet potatoes, this is around 3 or 4 medium sized potatoes. Place in a tea towel and squeeze out as much liquid as you can. It should measure around 2 1/4 cups after squeezing.

Stir through 1/4 cup chickpea flour and 1/2 a teaspoon salt, then add 3-4 tablespoons of vegan milk, stirring until evenly combined.

Brush a baking sheet with oil, then divide the mixture into 4, and spread each one thinly in a circle or love-heart. Bake for 20-25 minutes, flipping over for the last 5 minutes.

---

burgers with the lot

Gluten-Free Option, Soy Free Option,
Low Fat Option, Under 45 minutes Option

A healthy vegan version of the typical Australian chip shop burger, this works best with a mildly flavoured burger, to make the most of the toppings. The burger with the lot pictured on this page uses spicy aussie bbq baked soy-free tofu, from page 43.

To make burgers with the lot, prepare any burger or baked tofu recipe, along with some bread rolls, or baked hash browns and some cashew cheese. Sauté 1-2 onions per person over medium high heat until tender, then turn down heat to low and continue to stir every so often, until very soft and fragrant.

Spread the cashew cheese on the bread or hash browns, top with slices of fresh tomato (if in season), sautéed onion, sliced canned or boiled beetroot, salad and tomato or barbecue sauce.

Pineapple can be used in place of the beetroot for a delicious Hawaiian burger.

curried chickpea and sweet potato patties

These are patties in the "mushy but delicious" style of veggie burger. Great served with mango chutney or another Indian chutney, sweet chili sauce or ketchup. Serve as patties with sides of mashed potato, cauliflower, or pappadams, in wraps with salad greens, or as open-faced sandwiches like the ones in the photo.

Gluten-Free,
No Specialty Ingredients, Low Fat Option
No Nuts, Under 45 Minutes
Kitchen time 10-15 minutes
Serves 4

ingredients

water, for boiling
14oz (400g) sweet potato, cut into 3/4" (2cm) dice (2 1/3 cups after dicing)
1 tablespoon olive oil
3 cloves garlic, finely chopped (optional)
1 tablespoon finely chopped fresh ginger
1 medium-large onion, grated
1 teaspoon turmeric
1 teaspoon garam masala
1/2 teaspoon cumin
4 1/2 cups cooked chickpeas
1/4-1/2 teaspoon cayenne pepper
1/4-1/2 teaspoon salt
1 teaspoon lemon juice or apple cider vinegar

method

Bring a small pot of water to the boil. Add the sweet potato. Boil for around 15 minutes, or until mashable. Drain.

While the sweet potato is boiling, prepare the other ingredients.

Heat the oil in a frying pan over medium-high heat. When it is hot add the garlic, ginger and onion, stirring constantly until fragrant, around two minutes. Turn off the heat and stir through the turmeric, garam masala and cumin for 30 seconds, then add the chickpeas and stir through. Roughly mash the chickpeas with a fork until no whole chickpeas remain. Add the cooked sweet potato and throughly mash. Mix through the sweet potato, then adjust the seasonings with cayenne pepper, salt and lemon juice. Leave until cool enough to handle before forming into patties.

Form into heaped tablespoon sized patties, rolling in flour, vegan breadcrumbs, cornmeal or nut meal if you wish. Heat up 2-3 tablespoons of olive oil (or enough to coat the base of your frying pan) and fry at a medium-high heat on one side for 5 minutes, turn over and fry for a further 2 minutes. If you're cooking all 4 serves at once, you may need to fry them in two batches, or with a really big pan. Alternatively, for a lower fat option, brush the patties with oil and bake on a lined and greased baking sheet in the oven for 20 minutes.

not-köttbullar (swedish not-meatballs) with mashed potatoes and gravy

Hearty and savoury not-meatballs spiced with nutmeg, pepper and cloves, complimented by a side of creamy mashed potatoes and an umami-rich gravy.

No Nuts, Under 45 Minutes
Kitchen time 15-20 minutes
Total time 35 minutes
Serves 4

ingredients

water, for cooking potatoes
800g (1.75lb) potatoes

1 cup rolled oats
3/4 cup sunflower seeds
1/3 teaspoon ground cloves
1/2 teaspoon ground nutmeg
1 teaspoon cracked pepper
1 small-medium onion
2 tablespoons miso, tamari or coconut aminos
2 tablespoons vegan worcestershire sauce
2 tablespoons tomato sauce (ketchup)
4 1/2 cups cooked adzuki, borlotti or pinto beans*

for the gravy:
1 tablespoon olive oil
1 medium onion, diced
1 tablespoon flour
1 1/2 cups vegan milk
4 teaspoons vegan worcestershire sauce
4 teaspoons miso
2 teaspoons tomato sauce (ketchup)
1 teaspoon balsamic vinegar
1 teaspoon cracked pepper
a pinch of ground cloves
a pinch of ground nutmeg

*Use adzuki beans for best results. These are easier to find as dry beans rather than canned, and cook fairly quickly once they've been soaked.

Soy-free option: use a soy-free miso, or coconut aminos

method

Preheat the oven to 350f (175c). Grease two baking sheets.

Bring a pot of water to the boil for the potatoes. Chop the potatoes into roughly 1 inch (2.5cm) cubes. When the water is boiling, add the potatoes, bring back to the boil, reduce the heat and simmer for 20 minutes, or until fork-tender.

Process oats and sunflower seeds in a food processor until it resembles breadcrumbs, around 60 seconds. Place in a mixing bowl with the cloves, nutmeg and pepper. Stir to combine.

Remove the skin from the onion, chop into quarters and place in the food processor with the miso, worcestershire sauce and tomato sauce. Process until no large pieces of onion remain. Add the azduki beans to the processor and process until the uniform in colour. Add to the dry ingredients in the mixing bowl and stir until evenly combined.

For best results, leave the mixture to sit for a few minutes, or a few days if you wish. Take tablespoons of the mixture and roll into balls using your hands.

Place on the prepared baking sheets and bake for around 25 minutes.

To make the gravy:
Heat a tablespoon of olive oil in a frying pan. When it is hot, add the onion and sauté until tender and fragrant, a couple of minutes. Stir through the flour, then add the vegan milk, worcestershire sauce, miso, tomato sauce, balsamic vinegar and spices. Bring to the boil. Reduce the heat to the lowest setting until you wish to serve the gravy, or take off the heat and reheat it later.

When the not-meatballs have finished baking, drain the water from the potatoes and mash them up with some olive oil, vegan milk and salt, to taste.

bean and sunflower seed rissoles

With cooked beans on hand, these are a really fast and easy burger with a satisfying taste and texture. This recipe can be doubled or tripled and the mixture kept in the fridge for up to 5 days before cooking.

Nightshade Free
No Nuts, Under 45 Minutes
Kitchen time 10-15 minutes
Cooking time 7 minutes
Serves 2

ingredients

1 small onion, diced (very finely diced if you're not using a food processor)

2 cloves garlic, finely chopped

1/2 cup sunflower seeds

1 1/2 cups cooked beans (borlotti, pinto, azduki or cannellini)

2 1/2 tablespoons miso (or nutritional yeast, plus 1/2 teaspoon salt)

1 tablespoon vegan worcestershire sauce or coconut aminos

1/4 teaspoon dried rosemary

1/2 teaspoon dried thyme

1/2 teaspoon dried oregano

3/4 cup rolled oats

method

Heat a little oil in a frying pan over medium-high heat. Sauté the onion until tender and fragrant, around 5 minutes, then add the garlic and sunflower seeds and continue to sauté for another two minutes, until the sunflower seeds develop some colour.

Use a food processor or fork to mash the beans. Mix through the miso, worcestershire sauce and herbs. Mix or process through the onion mixture from the frying pan until evenly combined, then mix through the oats (if you're using a food processor, you may have to scrape down the sides to make sure the oats get evenly mixed in).

Clean out the frying pan, allowing the mixture to sit for a couple of minutes (or store in the fridge for up to 5 days).

Form the mixture into heaped-tablespoon sized patties. Brush or spray the frying pan with oil and heat up over medium-high heat. Add the patties and cook until browned on one side - around 5 minutes, flip over and cook for another two minutes.

bean and rice veggie burgers

Full of savoury goodness with a great texture that's sure to impress even the pickiest eaters, this burger mixture can also be rolled into heaped teaspoon sized balls and baked for use as not-meatballs. These are incredible served as an Australian 'Burger with the Lot', or as 'Heathy Junk Food Burgers' with cashew mayonnaise, pickles, lettuce, tomato sauce and cashew cheese.

Gluten-Free,
No Specialty Ingredients, Low Fat
No Nuts, Under 45 minutes
Kitchen time 20-25 minutes
Baking time 20-25 minutes
Serves 6-8

ingredients

1 tablespoon coconut oil, or other cooking oil
2 medium onions, diced
2 cloves of garlic, finely chopped
2 medium carrots or beetroots, or one of each, diced
1 medium-large potato, diced
4 1/2 cups cooked beans (azduki, black, borlotti or pinto)
2 tablespoons tomato sauce (ketchup)
1 tablespoon vegan worcestershire sauce*
1 teaspoon salt
1 teaspoon cracked pepper
2 1/4 cups cooked brown rice (preferably medium grain)

method

Preheat the oven to 350f (175c).

Heat the coconut oil in a chef pan or frying pan over medium-high heat. Add the onions and sauté for 5 minutes, or until soft and fragrant. Add the garlic, carrot, beetroot and potato and continue to sauté for another two minutes. Turn the heat down to low and leave, stirring every now and then while you prepare the rest of the ingredients.

In a food processor combine the beans, tomato sauce, worcestershire sauce, salt and pepper. Process until smooth, then place in a large mixing bowl.

Add the rice to the food processor and process until ground into smaller pieces, around half or a third of the size of the original grain. Add this to the mixing bowl with the beans.

Take the pan off the heat and add the onions, garlic, carrot, beetroot and potato to the food processor. Process until in slightly bigger pieces than the rice (but not too small). Add this mixture to the bowl with the rice and beans and stir to combine. Form into patties right away, or refrigerate the mixture for up to a week, or freeze the patties for up to a few months.

Form the mixture into heaped tablespoon sized patties and place on a lined or greased baking sheet. Bake for 20-25 minutes.

*If you don't have vegan worcestershire sauce, tamari, coconut aminos or miso are good replacements, but the teaspoon of salt may need to be reduced to half.

chickpea schnitzel patties

Versatile and savoury patties that are great with saurkraut and boiled potatoes, or chips and tomato sauce. These can also be used in parmigiana or any other recipe that calls for schnitzels.

Gluten-Free Option, Soy-Free Option,
Low Fat Option, Nightshade-Free Option,
Onion- and Garlic-Free Option
No Nuts, Under 45 minutes
Kitchen time 10 minutes
Serves 2-3

ingredients

1/4 cup chickpea flour

2 teaspoons rapadura, or another unrefined sugar

2-3 teaspoons dried sage

1/2-1 teaspoon dried thyme

1/2 teaspoon dried rosemary

1/2 teaspoon salt (optional, recommended if using nutritional yeast and no miso)

1/4 teaspoon cayenne pepper (omit for nightshade-free option)

optional 1/2 teaspoon dried kelp granules

2-3 tablespoons soy-free mellow light miso, or nutritional yeast (savoury yeast flakes)

1 clove garlic, finely chopped (omit for onion- and garlic-free option)

2 tablespoons apple cider vinegar or lemon juice

1 tablespoon tahini

1/4 cup water

2 1/4 cups cooked chickpeas

wholegrain flour, as needed (up to 10 tablespoons)

wholegrain flour or organic cornmeal, for coating

method

In a mixing bowl or food processor combine all the dry ingredients until evenly mixed and no lumps remain. Add the garlic, vinegar, tahini, water and chickpeas and process or mash until evenly blended. If needed, add a tablespoon at a time of a wholegrain flour, to help make the mixture firm (the amount will depend on how much moisture there is in the chickpeas).

Take heaped tablespoons of the mixture and roll in some flour. Press lightly to form patty shapes.

Coat the base of a frying pan with oil and heat it up. When the oil is hot add the schnitzels and cook until the bottoms are golden, around 2-5 minutes. Flip over and cook until the other side is golden.

For a low fat version, bake in the oven for 20 minutes instead of frying.

Soy-Free and Gluten-Free Options: Check that your miso is soy-free or gluten-free, or use nutritional yeast instead.

casseroles, loaves, pies and bakes

chickpea mornay

The classic creamy comforting pasta bake with sea vegetable flavoured chickpeas, savoury 'cheezy' sauce and a crunchy topping. This recipe can easily be doubled to serve a larger family, or for a second dish to keep in the fridge for baking later in the week.

Gluten-Free Option, Soy-Free
Low Fat Option
Nightshade-Free Option, No Nuts
Kitchen time 15-20 minutes
Baking time 30 minutes
Serves 3

ingredients

water, for boiling
8.8oz (250g) wholegrain pasta - spirals, penne or other shape
3/4 cup peas, corn, diced carrots or tiny broccoli florets
1/4 cup wakame, ripped up sushi nori, or other mild sea vegetable
1 1/2 cups cooked chickpeas
1/4 cup vegan milk, for the chickpeas
1 onion, diced
1/4 cup flour (wholemeal barley, spelt, wheat or gluten-free)
1/3 cup nutritional yeast (savoury yeast flakes)
1 3/4 cups vegan milk, for the sauce
1 tablespoon lemon juice or apple cider vinegar, optional
2 teaspoons dijon mustard, or other prepared mustard, optional
salt, to taste
1 teaspoon cracked pepper
1 cup crumbled potato chips, vegan breadcrumbs, nut or seed meal, for topping

method

Preheat the oven to 350f (175c).

Bring a pot of water to the boil over medium-high heat for the pasta.

While you're waiting for the water to boil, combine the wakame and chickpeas in a mixing bowl and roughly mash until no whole chickpeas remain. Stir in 1/4 cup vegan milk.

Cook the pasta according to the packet directions, adding the peas for the last minute of cooking. Drain.

To make the sauce, sauté the onion over medium-high heat until tender and fragrant. Stir through the flour and nutritional yeast, then add the vegan milk, half a cup at a time, stirring each addition in completely to ensure that no lumps form. Bring to the boil over medium-high heat while stirring constantly, then reduce the heat to low and continue to stir for a minute longer. Take off the heat, then adjust the seasonings with lemon juice, mustard, salt and pepper.

Reserve 1/4 cup of the sauce. Combine the pasta and peas with the remaining sauce, stirring to coat. In an 8x12" (20x30cm) lasagne pan, or similar shallow casserole dish, thoroughly cover the base with the pasta, leaving half of the pasta in the pot. Cover this layer of pasta with most of the chickpeas, then top with a thin layer of pasta. Sprinkle with the remaining chickpeas, then place the rest of the pasta over the top. Drizzle with the reserved 1/4 cup sauce and sprinkle with your choice of crumbly topping.

Bake for 30 minutes, until the topping is crispy and golden.

baked chard dolmathes
stuffed with quinoa, beans and herbs

This is an incredibly delicious meal that even quinoa-haters will enjoy. Brown rice can be substituted for the quinoa, just add the currants and cook according to the directions on page 11.

To serve the dolmathes, spread a layer of baba ganoush (page 93) or lemon cashew cream on a plate, top with the dolmathes and drizzle with the thyme oil.

Gluten-Free, Soy-Free
No Specialty Ingredients, Low Fat
Nightshade-Free
No Nuts, Under 45 minutes
Kitchen time 30 minutes
Baking time 15 minutes
Serves 3

ingredients

3/4 cup quinoa
1/4 cup currants, sultanas or raisins
1 1/2 - 1 3/4 cups water
18 medium or large sized leaves rainbow chard or silverbeet
1/4 cup sunflower seeds
1 onion, diced
2 cloves garlic, finely chopped
1 1/2 cups cooked adzuki beans or brown lentils
2 tablespoons finely chopped fresh parsley, optional
1 teaspoon fresh thyme leaves (or 1/4 teaspoon dried)
zest of one lemon
1/2 teaspoon salt, or to taste
juice of one lemon
1/3 cup water
olive oil, for brushing

method

For best results, thoroughly rinse, then soak the quinoa for 12 hours, rinse, drain and cook with the currants and 1 1/2 cups water. If working with unsoaked quinoa, use 1 3/4 cups of water.

Bring to the boil, reduce the heat and simmer for 15 minutes. Switch off the heat and leave it to stand for at least five minutes.

Preheat the oven to 350f (175c). Brush 2 or 3 baking dishes with oil.

Steam or boil the greens for 3-4 minutes, to make them easier to roll.

Toast the sunflower seeds in a dry skillet until golden. Remove from the pan.

Heat up some olive oil in the skillet, then add the onion. Sauté until tender and fragrant, around five minutes, then add the garlic, stirring for another minute or two. Add the quinoa, currants, beans, parsley and thyme, along with the lemon zest.

Pour the lemon juice and 1/3 cup water into the baking dishes.

Cut the tough parts of the stem out of the middle of the chard. Place 1 to 1 1/2 tablespoons of filling towards the top of each leaf, leaving around an inch of room on each side. Fold the sides over, and roll towards the base of the leaf, to seal completely. Place in the baking dishes, making sure the sides of the rolls are not touching. Brush the tops of the dolmathes with olive oil if you wish, then bake for around 15 minutes, until heated through.

thyme oil

1 tablespoon fresh thyme leaves
a pinch of salt
2 tablespoons olive oil
1/2 teaspoon lemon juice or apple cider vinegar

Crush the thyme with the salt in a pestle and mortar, add the olive oil and lemon juice.

lemon cashew cream

1 cup water
1 cup cashews
zest of half a lemon
1-2 teaspoons lemon juice

Combine all ingredients in a blender. For best results, leave to soak for a few minutes, or up to 8 hours before blending. Add extra lemon zest, to taste, if you like.

bean and vegetable pot pie

A creamy bean and vegetable filling subtly flavoured with herbs and topped with flaky pastry. This is the perfect food for a cold day and is great served on its own, or with some tomato sauce or ketchup. The filling and pastry will keep separately or pre-assembled in the fridge for up to a week.

Gluten-Free Option,
Nightshade-Free Option, No Nuts
Kitchen time 25-30 minutes
Cooking time 30 minutes
Makes 4 large serves

ingredients

For the pastry:

2 1/2 cups wholemeal flour (spelt, wheat or gluten-free)
1/4 teaspoon salt
1/3 cup olive or melted coconut oil
1/2 teaspoon apple cider vinegar or lemon juice
cold water, as needed (preferably iced)

For the filling:

2 medium potatoes (or swede (rutabaga), or parsnips)
2 medium carrots
1 medium-large onion
2 tablespoons wholemeal flour
2 cups vegan milk
2 teaspoons nutritional yeast (savoury yeast flakes)
1/2 teaspoon dried sage
1/4 teaspoon dried thyme
1/4 teaspoon dried rosemary
salt and cracked pepper, to taste
1 cup peas
3 cups cooked butter beans (lima beans), or other white bean

method

To make the pastry:
Combine the flour and salt in a mixing bowl. Drop spoonfuls of the oil and the vinegar into the mixing bowl, and then mix in quickly with your fingers until it resembles breadcrumbs. Add a little cold water at a time, mixing in until a dough forms. Cover and refrigerate while you prepare the rest of the recipe.

To make the filling:
Bring some water in a pot or steamer to the boil. Dice the potatoes and carrots and steam or boil for 10 minutes.

While the potatoes and carrots are steaming, dice the onion and sauté it in one or two tablespoons of oil over medium-high heat until tender and fragrant. Stir through the flour, then add the vegan milk, a little at a time, to form a sauce. Add the nutritional yeast, herbs, salt and pepper. Bring to the boil, then reduce the heat to low.

When the potatoes and carrots have finished, add these, along with the peas to the sauce, turn up the heat to medium-high and bring to the boil. Turn off the heat and gently stir through the butter beans.

Divide the mixture between four bowls. Divide the pastry into four pieces and press each one out with your hands to fit each bowl. Bake for 30 minutes, or until the pastry is cooked.

Nightshade-Free Option: Use swede (rutabaga) or parsnip instead of potatoes

cauliflower parmigiana bake

This casserole will convince any cauliflower haters that cauliflower can be really tasty. A great 'comfort food' style dish that is simple to make, and also low in fat and carbs, but you would never guess this from tasting it.

Gluten-Free Option,
Low Fat, No Nuts Option
Under 45 Minutes
Kitchen time 10 minutes
Baking time 30 minutes
Serves 2

ingredients

1.1lb (500g) cauliflower florets, cut into thin, even pieces (1 heaped dinner plate after chopping)

1 cup prepared tomato pasta sauce

1 1/2 cups cooked beans (adzuki, borlotti, pinto, cannellini, black eye, butter or red kidney)

1/4 cup flour (wholemeal spelt, wheat, barley, gluten-free, coconut or almond)

1/3 cup nutritional yeast (savoury yeast flakes)

optional 1-2 teaspoons olive or coconut oil

1/2-3/4 teaspoon salt, or to taste

1 1/2 cups vegan milk

optional 1/3 cup walnut meal, almond meal, sunflower seed meal or vegan breadcrumbs

method

Preheat the oven to 340f (170c).

Steam or boil the cauliflower florets for 5 minutes.

Make a cheezy sauce by combining the flour, nutritional yeast, olive oil and salt in a small saucepan and slowly mixing in the vegan milk, a little at a time. Bring to the boil over medium heat while stirring constantly. Reduce heat and simmer while stirring for another minute.

Place the pasta sauce in a gratin or casserole dish of at least a 1.16 quart (1.1 litre) capacity. Cover with the beans. Top with the cauliflower florets. Pour the cheezy sauce over the cauliflower, sprinkle with the walnut meal and bake for 30 minutes, or until bubbling.

baked spring rolls

Crispy on the outside with a delicious mildly-flavoured vegetable and bean sprout filling these are so healthy, hearty and full of protein that they can be enjoyed as a meal on their own. Best served with sweet chili sauce.

A food processor with a grating attachment makes light work of the preparation, but with a little extra time all the ingredients can be chopped and grated by hand. I generally make all the mixture, keep it in the fridge for up to five days and bake two serves at a time. They can also be rolled and then frozen, with no defrosting required (just a little extra baking time).

Gluten-Free Option, Soy-Free Option
No Specialty Ingredients
Low Fat, No Nuts
Preparation time 40 minutes
Baking time 25-35 minutes
Serves 6

ingredients

3 spring onions (green onions), finely chopped
1 clove garlic, finely chopped
1 tablespoon finely chopped fresh ginger
3 tablespoons miso, tamari or coconut aminos
1 tablespoon apple cider vinegar
1 teaspoon apple juice concentrate, agave or sugar
1 teaspoon finely chopped fresh or jarred chili, or 1/4 teaspoon cayenne pepper
4 3/4 cups mung bean sprouts
17.5oz (500g) daikon radish (or extra cabbage)
1 medium carrot
1/2 a medium green cabbage (17.5oz/500g)
optional 1 red capsicum (bell pepper) or a pinch of cayenne pepper

12-18 sheets mountain bread, tortillas or spring roll wrappers
cooking oil, for brushing
sesame seeds, for sprinkling

method

Preheat the oven to 350f (175c).

In a large mixing bowl, combine the spring onions, garlic, ginger, miso, vinegar, apple concentrate, chili and mung bean sprouts. Using a food processor, grate the radish, carrot, cabbage and capsicum. Add this to the mixing bowl with the other ingredients and mix until evenly combined.

Making this as 12 rolls (2 per serve) will make thicker rolls that should be eaten with a knife and fork, 18 smaller rolls (3 per serve) are great for eating without cutlery.

Take as many sheets of flatbread as you want to bake now and place on a clean surface for rolling up. Place some of the filling (3 tablespoons for small rolls, 4-5 for larger ones) towards one edge of the bread, leaving around half an inch (1 1/2cm) on each side. Roll up, folding the edges in as you go to form a sealed roll. Place seam side down on a lined or greased baking sheet. Repeat for the rest of the rolls, brush with oil and sprinkle with sesame seeds. Bake for 25-35 minutes, until crispy and golden.

Gluten-free option: make sure the flatbread and miso are gluten-free
Soy-free option: use soy-free miso, coconut aminos or soy-free tamari

lentil pastitsio

A hearty Greek pasta bake with a delicious tomato and lentil sauce sandwiched between layers of wholegrain pasta, topped with a creamy sauce and sprinkled with a crunchy topping.

Gluten-Free Option, Soy-Free Option, No Nuts Option,
Kitchen time 40 minutes
Baking time 25 minutes
Serves 4-6

ingredients

For the pasta layers:
water, for boiling
1.1lb (500g) wholegrain penne, macaroni or other small tube-shaped pasta
1/2 cup chickpea flour
2 tablespoons nutritional yeast
1/4 - 1/2 teaspoon salt
1/2 cup water

For the lentil and tomato layer:
1 large onion, finely chopped
4 cloves garlic, finely chopped
1.5lb (700g) tomato purée, or diced tomatoes
1/2 cup water (preferably lentil cooking water)
2 tablespoons red wine vinegar
2-3 tablespoons miso or tamari (or some salt, to taste)
optional 1/4 cup finely chopped sundried tomatoes
4 1/2 cups cooked lentils
1 1/2 teaspoons cinnamon
1 teasoon nutmeg
optional 2 tablespoons finely chopped parsley

For the white sauce:
7 tablespoons wholegrain flour
3 tablespoons nutritional yeast
a pinch or two of nutmeg
3 tablespoons olive oil
2 1/2 cups vegan milk
1 teaspoon apple cider vinegar or lemon juice
salt, to taste

For the crunchy topping:
1 1/4 cups sunflower seeds, walnuts or almond meal
1/3 cup nutritional yeast (savoury yeast flakes)
a pinch of salt

method

Preheat the oven to 350f (175c).

Bring a pot of water to the boil for the pasta. In a large mixing bowl combine the chickpea flour, water, nutritional yeast, salt and water. Cook the pasta according to the packet directions. Drain, then add to the mixing bowl and stir to coat in the chickpea flour batter.

While you're waiting for the pasta water to boil and the pasta to cook, prepare the lentil and tomato mixture by sautéing the onion over medium-high heat in some olive oil until tender and fragrant - around 5 minutes. Stir through the garlic for a few seconds, then add the tomato purée, water, vinegar, miso, sundried tomatoes, lentils, cinnamon, nutmeg and parsley. Bring to the boil. Reduce the heat and simmer while you prepare the white sauce and crunchy topping.

To make the white sauce, mix the flour, nutritional yeast and nutmeg in a medium saucepan. Stir through the oil, then add the vegan milk, a little at a time. Place over a medium-high heat and bring to the boil while stirring. Reduce the heat and simmer while stirring for a minute or two, until slightly thickened. Adjust the seasonings with salt and vinegar, this sauce should have some flavour but should not have too much salt. If in doubt, use less salt, not more.

To make the crunchy topping, combine the sunflower seeds, nutritional yeast and salt in a food processor. Process until crumbly. To make without a food processor use almond meal instead of the sunflower seeds.

To assemble, cover the base of two shallow 2 litre ovenproof dishes with the pasta mixture, leaving some for sprinkling over the tops. Cover the pasta with all of the lentil and tomato mixture, then sprinkle with the remaining pasta. Pour over the white sauce, then sprinkle with the crunchy topping

Bake uncovered for 25 minutes. Remove from the oven and allow to stand for 5 minutes before serving.

These will keep well in the fridge for a few days for baking later in the week if you wish. **67**

baked potatoes

For a simple meal, potatoes can be baked this way and topped with whatever toppings you have on hand. For high protein meals, always include at least half a cup of beans per serve as a topping. Pre-cooking the potatoes by boiling takes the guess work out of baking potatoes, resulting in potatoes that are fully cooked when they go into the oven, yet still end up with crispy skins and plenty of flavour, in far less time than it normally takes to bake them.

Gluten-Free, Soy-Free
No Specialty Ingredients
Low Fat, Onion- and Garlic-Free
No Nuts, Under 45 Minutes
Kitchen time 5-10 minutes
Cooking time 40-60 minutes

ingredients
water, for boiling
potatoes, around 300g (10oz) per serve
toppings and sauces of your choice

suggested toppings for 2 serves

Baked beans and greens (pictured on this page)
1 400g (14oz) tin baked beans
as much spinach, kale or other greens as you would like

Heat the beans on the stove, stir through the greens for a minute or two, until brightly coloured and wilted. Top the baked potatoes with this and serve right away.

Mexican
1 400g (14oz) tin vegan refried beans
Shredded lettuce and/or grated carrot
optional avocado and lemon or lime juice

Heat the refried beans, pour over the top of the baked potatoes, top with raw vegetables and sprinkle with lemon or lime juice.

Hummus, Beans and Salad
as much hummus or tahini sauce as you'd like
1 400g (14oz) tin 4 bean mix, rinsed and drained
salad leaves

Spread the hummus (page 94) or tahini sauce (page 96) on top of the potatoes. Rinse and drain the 4 bean mix, then place this, along with the salad leaves on the potatoes.

Pizza
pizza or pasta sauce
1 recipe pepperoni beans (page 96)
Pizza toppings that don't need cooking, eg: olives, pineapple, tomatoes, artichoke hearts, semidried tomatoes...

Heat up the pizza or pasta sauce, place this on top of the baked potatoes. Heat the bean pepperoni and place on top of the sauce. Sprinkle with your favourite pizza toppings and serve.

method
Bring a pot of water to the boil.

Preheat the oven to 390f (200c).

Wash the potatoes and add these to the boiling water. Boil with the lid on for 20-30 minutes, until fork-tender.

Drain the potatoes and place directly on an oven rack, or on a sheet of baking paper. Bake for around 20-30 minutes, until the skins are crispy. Prepare the toppings while the potatoes are baking.

Cut through the potatoes, open them up and mash with a fork, adding some coconut oil for best results. Top with your choice of toppings.

roasted vegetable frittata

A frittata is similar to a quiche, but without the crust. This one is full of the delicious flavours of roasted vegetables and is great served hot or cold. While it takes a long time to make if you include roasting the vegetables, most of that time is when it's cooking in the oven, so you could cook this for the next day's lunch while making dinner, or just roast the vegetables when you have a spare moment, and then assemble and bake it later. Made from pre-roasted vegetables it will take less than 45 minutes.

Gluten-Free, Soy Free, Low Fat,
Nightshade-Free option,
Onion- and Garlic-Free Option
No Nuts
Preparation time 10 -15 minutes
Total cooking time 70 minutes
Serves 4

ingredients

1.3lb (600g) sweet potato, pumpkin or winter squash
7oz (200g) potatoes (4 small ones), or other root vegetable
2 onions, sliced into thin wedges (optional)
1 red capsicum (red pepper)*, cut into 1/4" (1/2cm) strips
1 medium zucchini*, cut into 1/2" (1cm) thick circles
2 cups chickpea flour
1 1/2 - 2 teaspoons salt
optional 2 tablespoons nutritional yeast
optional 1/2 teaspoon cracked pepper
2 cups water

method

Preheat the oven to 350f (175c).

Cut the sweet potato and potatoes into 1/2" (1cm) thick slices. Place on a baking sheet and toss them in some oil if you wish (or bake without oil on a lined baking sheet). Bake for 20 minutes, then flip each piece over. Bake for another 15 minutes.

While the sweet potato and potato are baking, prepare the capsicum, onion and zucchini on a separate baking sheet, using oil or a lined sheet. Bake for 15 minutes.

In a mixing bowl combine the chickpea flour, salt and nutritional yeast, crushing it up if there are any lumps. Mix in the water a little at a time to avoid any lumps forming.

Grease an 8x12" (20x30cm) lasagne pan or casserole dish. Place all of the potatoes and sweet potato at the bottom of the dish, covering as much of the base as possible. Pour in the chickpea flour mixture, then scatter the remaining vegetables evenly on top. Bake for around 35 minutes, or until the middle of the frittata is set. Leave to stand for at least five minutes before cutting out pieces and serving. Serve hot or cold with a green salad.

*If capsicum and zucchini are not in season other vegetables such as cauliflower and broccoli can be used instead of the zucchini, and some preroasted capsicum, semi-dried tomatoes, artichoke hearts or olives from a jar can be sprinkled on top of the frittata after the other vegetables have been roasted.

pea and cauliflower samosa pot pies

All the delicious taste of samosas but without the hassle of making small pastries - with the added nutritional benefits of cauliflower and lots of peas for protein.

Gluten-Free Option, Soy-Free
No Specialty Ingredients
Nightshade-Free Option, No Nuts
Under 45 Minutes
Kitchen time 15 -20 minutes
Baking time 25-30 minutes
Serves 4

ingredients

For the filling:
4 cups cauliflower florets (1.3lb/600g)
3 teaspoons brown or black mustard seeds
2 teaspoons cumin seeds
optional 1/2 teaspoon fennel seeds
1 tablespoon oil (coconut or olive)
1 medium/large onion, finely chopped
1 tablespoon finely chopped fresh ginger
2 cloves garlic, finely chopped
1 teaspoon turmeric
1 teaspoon garam masala
1/4 teaspoon cumin
4 cups peas
1 1/2 cups water
1/4 teaspoon cayenne pepper, optional
salt, to taste

For the pastry:
2 1/2 cups wholemeal flour (spelt, wheat or gluten-free)
1/4 teaspoon salt
1/3 cup olive oil
1/2 teaspoon apple cider vinegar or lemon juice
cold water, as needed

oil, for brushing
optional nigella or black cumin seeds, for sprinkling

method
Preheat the oven to 350f (175c).

To make the filling:
Steam the cauliflower until it is tender and breaks apart easily with a fork, around 10-12 minutes.

While the cauliflower is steaming, prepare the spices, along with the onion, garlic and ginger.

Place the mustard, cumin and fennel seeds in a dry frying pan over medium heat. Stir every now and then until they begin to make popping sounds, then add a tablespoon of oil, along with the onion. Sauté until tender and fragrant, around 4 minutes, then stir through the garlic, ginger, turmeric, garam masala and cumin. Continue to stir for another minute, then add the peas, water, cayenne pepper and steamed cauliflower. Roughly mash the cauliflower, bring to the boil and cook until the peas are heated through, around 2 minutes. Add salt, to taste.

To make the pastry:
Combine the flour and salt in a mixing bowl. Drop spoonfuls of the oil and the vinegar into the mixing bowl, and then mix in quickly with your fingers until it resembles breadcrumbs. Add a little cold water at a time, mixing it in until a dough forms.

To assemble:
Place the filling into four separate bowls of at least 1 1/2 cups capacity each. Divide the pastry into four pieces and use your hands to press each piece into a circle that will cover the filling. Put the pastry on top of the filling, pressing to the edges of the bowl to seal. Make a small hole for steam to escape with a knife or fork, then brush with oil and sprinkle with seeds if you wish. Bake for 25-30 minutes.

lentil loaf

A hearty centrepiece for a roast meal in under 45 minutes. The mixture makes enough for 3 loaves (2 big serves per loaf) and keeps well in the fridge for up to a week.

ingredients

1 1/2 cups red lentils
3 cups water
2/3 cup sunflower seeds*
2 3/4 cups rolled oats
1/2 teaspoon dried thyme
1/2 teaspoon dried oregano
1/2 teaspoon rosemary
1/4 teaspoon cayenne pepper
1 1/2 teaspoons salt (reduce if using tamari instead of worcestershire sauce)
1 1/2 cups cooked cannellini beans, or other beans
2 medium onions
5 tablespoons tomato sauce or ketchup
4 tablespoons vegan worcestershire sauce (or tamari or coconut aminos)
optional 2 tablespoons balsamic vinegar
olive oil, for drizzling on top

For the optional topping:
6 tablespoons tomato sauce or ketchup
3 tablespoons vegan worcestershire sauce

*If you don't have a food processor, use almond meal in place of the sunflower seeds, thoroughly mash the cannellini beans and grate the onion.

No Specialty Ingredients Option
No Nuts, Under 45 Minutes
Kitchen time 15 minutes
Total time 45 minutes
Serves 6

method

Preheat the oven to 175c (350f).

Bring the lentils and the water to the boil. Reduce the heat and simmer for 10 minutes. Turn off the heat and leave to sit for at least 5 minutes.

If you're making roast vegetables, get these in the oven while the lentils are cooking.

In a food processor*, grind the sunflower seeds until crumbly (about a minute). Add 1 cup of the oats and grind for another 30 seconds. Place this mixture in a large bowl with the rest of the oats, along with the thyme, oregano, rosemary, cayenne pepper and salt.

Place the cannellini beans, onions, tomato sauce, worcestershire sauce and vinegar in the food processor* and blend until no large pieces remain. Add this and the lentils to the mixing bowl with the dry ingredients and stir to combine.

Divide the mixture into 3, making one loaf from each third of the mix. The leftover mixture can be refrigerated for up to a week if you don't want to make all three loaves at once.

Using the same tray as the roasted vegetables (or another greased tray) form a long and fairly flat loaf (around 25cm/10" long, 2.5cm/1" tall and 7.5cm/3" wide). Drizzle with a little olive oil and bake for 25-30 minutes, until firm and cooked through (if using the topping, bake for 15 minutes, then spread the topping over the top of the loaf, smooth it out with a spoon and bake for 10-15 more minutes).

lancashire hot pot

While a traditional Lancashire hot pot is baked for a longer time than what my recipe uses, this one is still full of flavour with slow-baked textures and savoury goodness.

Gluten-Free Option
Soy-Free Option
No Specialty Ingredients
Low Fat Option, No Nuts
Kitchen time 15-20 minutes
Baking time 75 minutes
Serves 2

ingredients

2 medium onions, sliced into half moons
1 small onion, diced
2 teaspoons flour (wholemeal barley, spelt, wheat or gluten-free)
1 cup bean cooking water, or plain water
3 tablespoons vegan worcestershire sauce, coconut aminos, tamari or miso
1 tablespoon balsamic vinegar
a tiny pinch of dried thyme, or 1/2 teaspoon fresh
1 teaspoon cracked pepper
salt, to taste
2 cups cooked azduki, borlotti or pinto beans
2 medium-large potatoes, thinly sliced (around 14oz (400g))

method

Preheat the oven to 340f (170c).

For best results, use a dish that can be used on the hotplate as well as the oven. If you don't have a suitable dish it will still taste great made in separate dishes.

Sauté the onion half moons in some oil over medium-high heat until tender and fragrant, around 5 minutes. Place in a bowl and set aside until later.

Return the pan to heat with a little more oil if needed and sauté the diced onion until fragrant, around 4 minutes. Stir through the flour, then pour in the water, worcestershire sauce and balsamic vinegar. Bring to the boil. Add thyme and pepper, and salt to taste, remembering that the flavours will intensify in the oven so it's better to use less salt rather than too much. Add the beans and bring to the boil again. Take off the heat.

If your pot is ovenproof, simply top the bean mixture with the onion half moons, then the potato slices. Drizzle with olive oil if you wish and sprinkle with a couple of pinches of salt. Bake with the lid on (or some foil) for 45 minutes.

If your pot is not ovenproof, just pour the bean mixture into an ovenproof dish and top with the onions and potatoes, cover and cook in the same way.

Once the hot pot has baked for 45 minutes with the lid on, take the lid off and bake it for another 30-40 minutes, or until the potatoes are golden.

tostadas

These are a fantastic eat-with-your-hands lunch. The natural flavour of the black beans is complimented perfectly by spicy guacamole, crisp lettuce and the optional addition of vegan cheese, served up on a freshly fried tortilla. I like to make these with freshly cooked black beans and the homemade tortilla recipe below, but for a faster recipe you could use shop-bought tortillas and canned beans.

No Specialty Ingredients Option
No Nuts Option
Total kitchen time: 45-55 minutes
Total time: 50-60 minutes
(not including bean soaking and cooking time)
Serves 2

ingredients

6-14 small tortillas
oil, for shallow frying
2 cups cooked black beans
1 recipe guacamole
optional cashew cheese
2 cups shredded lettuce

cashew cheese

3/4 cup cashews
1/2 cup water
1/2 cup nutritional yeast
1 teaspoon apple cider vinegar
optional 1 teaspoon agave
1/2 teaspoon salt

For best results soak the cashews in the water before blending, for as little as a few minutes or as long as 8 hours.

In a blender or food processor, combine all the ingredients on a low setting. Increase the speed to the highest setting after 20 seconds then blend for another 2 minutes or so, until smooth. This will thicken in the fridge.

guacamole

1 big ripe avocado
juice of half a lime or lemon (add the juice from the other half if you like)
2 spring onions (green onions), finely chopped (or 1/4 cup finely diced red onion)
optional 1 or 2 tomatoes, diced
1/2 teaspoon cumin, or to taste
1/4 teaspoon salt, or to taste
1/4 teaspoon cayenne pepper, or to taste

Halve the avocado, remove the stone, scoop out the insides and place them in a bowl. Stir though the lime juice, then add the onions and tomatoes. Adjust the spices and salt to your preference, adding extra lime juice if you wish.

method

If you wish to make your own tortillas, follow the directions on this page. While the dough is resting, prepare the other parts of the meal, then roll out the tortillas, fry and serve.

To fry the tortillas:
Heat 1/4" (1/2cm) oil in a frying pan. When the oil is hot, add one tortilla and fry until the bottom is golden and firm, flip over and fry the other side. Remove from the pan and repeat for the rest of the tortillas.

To assemble the tostadas:
Spread a tortilla with cashew cheese or guacamole. Top with a layer of black beans, then a layer of lettuce, and finish with some guacamole. These can be served pre-assembled, or as a 'make-your-own' meal, with all the components served separately at the table.

wheat and corn tortillas

Makes 14 (2-3 large serves)
1 1/2 cups wholemeal wheat flour
1 cup cornmeal (polenta)*
1/2- 1 teaspoon salt
1 tablespoon olive oil
1 cup water, or more, as needed
extra flour, for rolling
oil, for shallow frying

In a mixing bowl combine the wheat flour, cornmeal and salt. Add the olive oil and rub it into the flour with your fingers, to evenly distribute it. Add the water, first mixing with a spoon, and then kneading with your hands for a minute or two. It should form a dough and not break apart too easily, nor be too wet either. Cover and leave to sit for at least 15 minutes, preferably 8 hours.

Divide the mixture into 14 balls. Roll each one in some flour and use a rolling pin on a flat surface to roll them out into thin circles around 4-5" (10-13cm) wide. To stack them before frying, sprinkle a little flour between each tortilla, then top with the next one. Make 4 separate stacks, to minimise the risk of tortillas sticking to each other from the weight.

75

*the cornmeal shouldn't be too finely ground, it should have a grainy texture.

spinach and 'ricotta' calzones

A classic nutritious combination of greens with creamy, cheezy homemade vegan ricotta inside a thin and crispy pizza dough. Best served with a tomato sauce, relish or ketchup.

Soy Free Option, Nightshade-Free
Onion- and Garlic-Free
No Nuts Option
Kitchen time 10-15 minutes
Baking time 25-30 minutes
Serves 2-3

ingredients

For the dough:
1/4 cup water, for boiling
1/2 cup cold water
3 teaspoons fresh yeast, or 1 1/2 teaspoons dried yeast*
optional teaspoon of unrefined sugar
1 tablespoon olive oil
1 1/2 cups wholemeal wheat flour
1/4 cup cornmeal (polenta), or more wheat flour
optional tablespoon gluten
1/2 teaspoon salt

For the 'ricotta':
1/2 cup cashews or sunflower seeds*
1/3 cup water
2 tablespoons lemon juice
optional teaspoon agave
2 tablespoons nutritional yeast (savoury yeast flakes)
optional 1/2 teaspoon miso
1/2 teaspoon salt
1 1/2 cups cooked cannellini beans, or other white beans

1/3-1/2 small bunch silverbeet (chard) or spinach, finely chopped (2-3 packed cups after chopping)

method

To make the dough: Bring 1/4 cup water to the boil. Take off the heat and add 1/2 cup cold water, along with the yeast, sugar and oil.

In a mixing bowl combine the wholemeal wheat flour, cornmeal, gluten and salt. Add the water, yeast, sugar and oil to this, stirring to combine. Knead for 2-5 minutes, until the dough develops some elasticity.

Leave to rise for 30-60 minutes in an oiled mixing bowl.

Preheat the oven to 400f (205c). Grease or line two baking sheets.

Combine the cashews, water, lemon juice, agave, nutritional yeast, miso and salt in a blender. Leave to sit for a couple of minutes, or up to 8 hours, then blend until the cashews are finely chopped and the mixture is creamy. Add the cannellini beans and blend until mixed through.

Put the spinach in a large mixing bowl and stir through the 'ricotta' until all the greens are thoroughly coated.

Divide the dough into 6 pieces. Roll each one into a ball, flatten and then stretch as thinly it will go without breaking. Place 3 of these on each baking sheet. Divide the spinach and 'ricotta' mixture in between each circle, stretch the edges of the dough out, brush with water and gently fold in half to form a semicircle. Press the edges to seal, then prick the top with a fork so steam can escape. Repeat for the remaining calzones.

Brush with oil and bake in the oven for 25-30 minutes, or until the edges are golden-brown.

*for an slow rise version of the dough, use only 1 teaspoon of fresh yeast (1/2 teaspoon dried) and leave to rise for 8-16 hours.

*If you don't have a blender, you can replace the cashews and water with 1/2 cup coconut cream and mash the beans instead.

slow rise spelt loaves

This simple, tasty and nutritious recipe makes it possible for a really busy person to make all their own bread. Wholemeal spelt flour is generally higher in protein than wheat flour, but if you prefer to use wholemeal wheat flour simply increase the amount of water by half a cup. For the most accurate results measuring the flour for this recipe, pour the flour into a measuring cup rather than scooping it out.

No Specialty Ingredients
Low Fat, Nightshade-Free
Onion- and Garlic-Free, No Nuts
Kitchen time 5-10 minutes
Rising time 24 hours
Baking time 35 minutes
Makes 2 medium loaves

ingredients

1/3 teaspoon fresh yeast, or 1/6 teaspoon dried yeast
3 1/2 cups cold water
7 cups wholemeal spelt flour
2 teaspoons salt
Sesame seeds, pumpkin seeds, sunflower seeds, cornmeal or semolina, for coating the loaves

method

In a large mixing bowl, dissolve the yeast in 3 cups of cold water. Stir through 4 cups of spelt flour, cover with a tea towel and leave to sit at room temperature for around 12 hours (anywhere from 6 to 24 hours is fine).

Stir the salt and the remaining 1/2 cup of water into the bowl. Add the remaining 3 cups of flour, stirring, then briefly kneading to make sure that it's evenly mixed through. Cover with a tea towel and leave to sit at room temperature for around 12 hours.

When you're ready to bake the bread, place a pizza stone in the oven and heat it up to 250c (480f) or as hot as your oven will go.

Cover a dinner plate in the seeds of your choice (or cornmeal, or semolina), divide the dough into two. Take one half of the dough and stretch it into a circle large enough to cover the seeds. Fold up two of the edges, to form a log. Repeat for the other half of the dough. Place the logs seam-side down on the pizza stone, slash with a bread knife, reduce the oven temperature to 220c (430f) and bake for around 35 minutes, until the loaves feel light when picked up and sound hollow when tapped on the bottom.

mushroom sandwiches with garlic and white bean spread

A delicious combination of savoury, juicy mushrooms with a garlicy bean spread and peppery rocket (although if you don't have rocket (arugula), you could substitute it with watercress, or another salad green).

Gluten-Free Option, Soy-Free,
No Specialty Ingredients
Nightshade-Free, No Nuts
Under 45 Minutes
Total time 15 minutes
Serves 2

ingredients

For the mushrooms:
2 tablespoons olive oil
1 1/2 tablespoons balsamic vinegar
1-2 cloves garlic, finely chopped
200g (7oz) mushrooms (around 3 large ones)

For the white bean spread:
1 tablespoon olive oil
1-2 cloves garlic, finely chopped
1 1/2 cups cooked cannellini beans, or other white beans
optional 2 tablespoons nutritional yeast (savoury yeast flakes)
salt, to taste

thin slices of bread (I use 10 small slices of homemade bread)
rocket (arugula) or watercress, to serve

method

Combine the olive oil, balsamic vinegar and garlic in a small bowl and whisk to combine. Remove the stems from the mushrooms and place gill-side up on a plate. Pour the oil, vinegar and garlic marinade over the top of each one. Toss the mushroom stems around in the bowl, to coat in the remaining marinade. Set aside while you prepare the white bean spread.

Heat the tablespoon of olive oil in a small saucepan. When it is hot, add the garlic and stir constantly until lightly browned - around a minute or two. Stir through the beans, and then mash. Add nutritional yeast and salt, to taste.

Heat a grill pan or large frying pan over medium-high heat. When it is hot, brush with oil and place the mushrooms on it. Cook until one side is seared (around 3-5 minutes), then flip over and cook the other side.

Alternatively the mushrooms can be sliced before cooking and sautéed in plenty of olive oil until fragrant. This is the best method if using small mushrooms.

Spread the white bean spread on all the bread slices. Top half of the slices with rocket. Remove the mushrooms from the pan and cut into thin slices. Place on top of the rocket, then cover with the remaining slices of bread.

chickpea and gherkin smørrebrød

Smørrebrød is a Danish open-faced sandwich, and is perfect for using slices of hearty wholegrain bread that aren't so great for using in two-slice sandwiches. In Denmark it's traditionally made from a dark rye sourdough, but I use my slow rise spelt or wheat bread (page 77) with great results. Traditionally butter is spread on the bread (that's what 'smørre' means), but I've used homemade vegan mayonnaise on this one.

Gluten-Free Option,
No Specialty Ingredients
Nightshade-Free, Onion- and Garlic-Free
Under 45 Minutes
Total time 5-10 minutes
Serves 2

ingredients

4-6 slices fresh wholemeal bread (preferably rye, or the bread recipe from this book)
homemade vegan mayonnaise (eg. cashew mayonnaise, recipe below)
salad greens, to serve
1 1/2 cups cooked chickpeas
pickled gherkin slices

method

Spread some vegan mayonnaise on the bread. Mix the salad greens with some more vegan mayo and place this on top of the bread. Using a fork, mash the chickpeas with plenty of vegan mayonnaise and cover the salad greens with this. Top with gherkin slices and serve right away.

cashew mayonnaise

1 cup raw cashews
1 cup water
1 tablespoon apple cider vinegar
1/4 cup vegan milk
1/4 - 1/2 cup olive oil
salt and pepper to taste (I use around half a teaspoon of each)

In a blender, soak the cashews in the water and vinegar for at least a couple of minutes, or up to 12 hours. Blend until smooth, then blend in the vegan milk. Slowly drizzle in the olive oil while blending. Add salt and pepper to taste. This will keep in the fridge for up to a week.

turkish flatbreads
with spicy tomato and bean topping

These flatbreads feature an incredibly delicious tomato and bean topping. If you've never used sumac before then it's worth seeking it out just for this recipe because it adds a really special touch to these breads when sprinkled over the top after baking. For a fast and easy meal the tomato and bean topping is also great spread on top of fresh or toasted bread and grilled (broiled).

No Nuts
Under 45 minutes option
Kitchen time 25 minutes
Baking time 20 minutes
Serves 2

ingredients

For the bread:
1/4 teaspoon fresh yeast, or 1/8 teaspoon dried*
1 1/4 cups cold water
3 cups wholemeal wheat flour
1/2 teaspoon salt

For the topping:
1 tablespoon olive oil
1 medium onion, finely diced
2 cloves garlic, finely chopped
1 1/2 cups cooked beans, mashed (adzuki, borlotti or pinto)
3 tablespoons tomato purée
1 tablespoon sugar
1/4 teaspoon cayenne pepper
1 teaspoon paprika
1/4 teaspoon salt, or to taste
optional 1/4 teaspoon black pepper
1 small bunch fresh parsley, finely chopped
1-2 teaspoons sumac
1 lemon, cut into wedges

method

Dissolve the yeast in a mixing bowl with the water. Add the flour and salt and knead to combine. Leave to rise for around 12 hours*.
To make the topping, heat the oil in a frying pan over medium-high heat. Sauté the onion until tender and fragrant, then stir through the garlic. Remove from the heat and add the beans, tomato purée, sugar, cayenne pepper, paprika, salt and pepper.

Preheat the oven to 410f (210c).

Oil 2 baking sheets. Punch the dough down, briefly knead, then divide into 4 pieces. Shape into balls, then flatten and stretch out on the baking sheets to less than 1cm (1/2") thick.

Cover the flatbreads with a thin layer of the bean mixture, spreading it right to the edges. Drizzle with a little olive oil if you wish.

Bake for 20 minutes, until cooked. Serve sprinkled with parsley, sumac and lemon juice. Fold in half, stuff with leafy greens if you like and eat as a sandwich, or enjoy as mini pizzas.

*for a faster option with the dough, use 2 teaspoons fresh yeast, or 1 teaspoon dried, and leave to rise for an hour.

pumpkin seed, lentil and herb sausages

A savoury sausage reminiscent of a typical Australian sausage - mildly flavoured and perfect for drenching in tomato sauce or serving with saurkraut.

Soy Free Option
Onion- and Garlic-Free Option
No Nuts
Kitchen time 10-15 minutes
Cooking time 45 minutes
Serves 4

ingredients

1 1/2 cups gluten (vital wheat gluten)
1/3 cup chickpea flour (besan)
1/2 cup pumpkin seeds, ground or chopped into small pieces
3 tablespoons nutritional yeast (savoury yeast flakes)
1 1/2 teaspoons dried rosemary, or 2 tablespoons fresh
1/4 teaspoon dried thyme, or 1 teaspoon fresh
1/4 teaspoon dried oregano, or 1 teaspoon fresh
1 teaspoon salt
1 teaspoon black pepper, ground
optional 1/2 teaspoon smoked paprika
1/4 teaspoon cayenne pepper

1 cup cooked lentils, or other beans
2 tablespoons olive or melted coconut oil
2 tablespoons vegan worcestershire sauce
1 cup water

method

Mix the dry ingredients in a mixing bowl until evenly combined.

In a measuring jug or separate bowl combine the olive oil, worcestershire sauce and water. Add this along with the lentils and mix in to the dry ingredients. Knead until all the dry ingredients are mixed in, adding extra water if you have to.

Prepare 8 or 12 pieces of baking paper or foil roughly three inches wide by eight inches long (7.5cm x 20cm). Divide the sausage mixture into 8 or 12 pieces, rolling each one roughly into a sausage shape and place each one lengthwise on a sheet of baking paper. Roll up and twist the ends, place in a steamer. Repeat for the remaining pieces.

Bring plenty of water to the boil in a saucepan and place the steamer on top of this. Steam for 40 minutes. Remove the sausages from the baking paper when you want to use them and fry, grill or broil until browned in places. Sausages can be refrigerated for up to a week after steaming or frozen for a few months before steaming.

Soy-free option: check that your worcestershire sauce is soy free, or reduce the salt by half and replace the sauce with coconut aminos

käsekrainer (aka 'kransky')

Smokey seitan sausages flavoured with garlic and black pepper, surrounding a delicious centre of vegan cheese. Best served with mustard.

Kitchen time 15-20 minutes
Cooking time 45 minutes
Serves 4

ingredients

2 teaspoons black pepper, ground
3 teaspoons smoked paprika
1 1/2 cups gluten (vital wheat gluten)
1/2 cup chickpea flour
3 tablespoons nutritional yeast (savoury yeast flakes)

1/2 teaspoon salt
4 big cloves garlic
2 tablespoons olive oil or melted coconut oil
1/2 cup tomato sauce (ketchup)
1 1/2 cups cooked beans (adzuki, borlotti or pinto)
2 tablespoons vegan worcestershire sauce, tamari,
        miso or coconut aminos
3/4 cup water

cashew cheeze (recipe below), for filling

method

In a large mixing bowl, combine the pepper, paprika, gluten, chickpea flour and nutritional yeast.

Place the salt and garlic in a mortar and pestle and crush until it turns into a paste (if you don't have one, you can just cut the garlic into really tiny pieces using a knife). Add this to a smaller bowl, along with the oil, tomato sauce, beans and worcestershire sauce. Mash or food process until the beans are evenly mushed up, then add 3/4 cup of water to this mixture. Mix through, then pour into the dry ingredients and stir, then knead to combine. Knead for another minute or two.

Bring a pot of water for the steamer to the boil. Divide the mixture into 8 pieces. Take 8 pieces of baking paper or foil roughly 3 inches wide by 8 inches long (7.5cm x 20cm). Take each piece of the sausage mixture and shape into a thick rectangle, around 4-5 inches long by 2 inches wide. Place 2 flat teaspoons of cashew cheeze in the length of this rectangle, leaving an inch around the edges. Fold the edges over to seal, then roll up to completely cover the cheeze. Roll up the baking paper and twist the ends, place in a steamer and repeat for the other 8 pieces.

Steam for 40 minutes. Remove sausages from the baking paper and fry in a little oil until browned in places. Sausages can be refrigerated for up to a week after steaming or frozen for a few months before steaming.

cashew cheeze

3/4 cup cashews
1/2 cup water
1/2 cup nutritional yeast
1 teaspoon apple cider vinegar
optional 1 teaspoon agave
1/2 teaspoon salt

For best results, soak the cashews in the water before blending for as little as a few minutes or as long as 8 hours.

In a blender or food processor, combine all the ingredients on a low setting. Increase the speed to the highest setting after 20 seconds then blend for another 2 minutes or so, until smooth. This will thicken in the fridge and is best made in advance for this recipe.

frankfurter (hot dogs)

A typical 'hot dog' style sausage, to serve with your favourite hot dog condiments. Mustard goes especially well with these.

Onion- and Garlic-Free
No Nuts
Kitchen time 10-15 minutes
Cooking time 45 minutes
Serves 4

ingredients

5 teaspoons smoked paprika
optional 1/4 teaspoon cayenne pepper
1/2 cup chickpea flour
3 tablespoons nutritional yeast (savoury yeast flakes)
1 1/2 cups gluten (vital wheat gluten)
1/2 teaspoon salt (omit if using miso or tamari)

1 1/2 cups cooked beans (borlotti, pinto or adzuki)
2 tablespoons olive oil or melted coconut oil
1/2 cup tomato sauce (ketchup)
2 tablespoons vegan worcestershire sauce, tamari, miso
       or coconut aminos
3/4 cup water

method

Bring a pot of water for the steamer to the boil.

In a mixing bowl, combine the paprika, cayenne pepper, chickpea flour, nutritional yeast, gluten and salt. Mix to combine, crushing any lumps of flour.

In a separate bowl or food processor, mash or process the beans until evenly mushed up. Add the olive oil, tomato sauce, worcestershire sauce and water and stir until evenly mixed. Pour this into the dry ingredients and mix with a spoon, then knead, until no traces of the dry ingredients remain.

Take 12 pieces of baking paper or foil roughly three inches wide by eight inches long (7.5cmx20cm). Divide the sausage mixture into 12 pieces and shape each one into a sausage shape. Place on a sheet of baking paper and roll up, twisting the ends to seal. Place in the steamer. Repeat for the remaining pieces.

Steam for 40 minutes. Remove the sausages from the baking paper when you wish to use them and grill, broil, barbecue or fry until browned in places. Sausages can be refrigerated for up to a week after steaming. If you only have a small steamer the sausages can be steamed 6 at a time, with the other half of the uncooked mixture keeping in the fridge for up to a week. Uncooked sausages can also be frozen for a few months before steaming.

dagwood dogs

Smokey seitan sausages in a crispy coating. Best served with lots of tomato sauce (ketchup) with oven chips and salad as side dishes.

Onion- and Garlic-Free
No Nuts
Kitchen time 10-15 minutes
Cooking time 45 minutes
Serves 2

ingredients

4 vegan frankfurter sausages* (see opposite page)
1/2 cup cornmeal (polenta)
1/2 cup boiling water
1/3 cup vegan milk
2 tablespoons olive oil (or other cooking oil)
3/4 cup barley flour (or other wholegrain flour)
1/4 cup chickpea flour (or extra barley flour)
1 teaspoon baking powder
1/4 teaspoon salt
extra barley flour, for rolling the sausages in
oil, for frying

method

Combine the cornmeal and boiling water in a small mixing bowl. Leave to stand for 5-10 minutes, so the corn can absorb the water, then add the vegan milk and olive oil.

In a larger mixing bowl combine the chickpea flour, barley flour, baking powder and salt. Mix until combined, then mix through the cornmeal mixture to form a thick batter. Place the batter on a plate.

Coat the base of a pan with at least 1/2" (1 1/2cm) oil. Heat it up over a medium-high heat while you coat the sausages in batter (alternatively, preheat the oven to 350f (175c)).

Sprinkle the extra flour on a plate. Roll the sausages in the flour, then place a skewer or stick through each one if you wish. Coat each sausage in the cornmeal batter, then roll again through the flour.

Fry each dagwood dog in the oil until golden on one side, then flip over and fry the other side, or drizzle with oil and bake for 30 minutes, flipping over for the last 10 minutes.

*If you're extra hungry and haven't steamed the sausages yet, you can shape the mixture into 8 larger sausages instead of 12 smaller ones, and the batter will be sufficient to coat 4 of these.

bratwurst

A vegan take on a traditional spiced bratwurst. Serve with saurkraut or sautéed onions, and a potato side dish or bread. These also taste great with mustard.

Soy-Free Option
Onion- and Garlic-Free
No Nuts
Kitchen time 10-15 minutes
Cooking time 45 minutes
Serves 4

ingredients

1 teaspoon caraway seeds
1 teaspoon black peppercorns
1 teaspoon coriander seeds
1/2 - 1 teaspoon salt
2 teaspoons yellow mustard seeds
1/2 teaspoon ground nutmeg
2 teaspoons oregano
optional 1/2 teaspoon smoked paprika
1 1/2 cups gluten (vital wheat gluten)
1/3 cup chickpea flour
2 tablespoons nutritional yeast (savoury yeast flakes)

1 1/2 cups cooked borlotti, pinto, adzuki or black beans
2/3 cup (packed) saurkraut (or finely chopped cabbage, plus a pinch or two of salt)
2 tablespoons tomato sauce (ketchup)
2 tablespoons vegan worcestershire sauce, tamari*, coconut aminos or miso*
2 tablespoons olive or melted coconut oil
1 cup water

method

Combine the caraway seeds, peppercorns, coriander and salt in a pestle and mortar (or spice grinder) and crush.

Add to a mixing bowl with the mustard seeds, nutmeg, oregano, paprika, gluten, chickpea flour and nutritional yeast, and stir to combine.

In a food processor or separate mixing bowl, process or mash the beans. Process or finely chop the saurkraut, then add the tomato sauce, worcestershire sauce, olive oil and water.

Pour the wet mixture into the dry ingredients and stir, then knead to combine.

Prepare 8 pieces of baking paper or foil roughly three inches wide by eight inches long (7.5cmx20cm). Divide the sausage mixture into 8 pieces, rolling each one roughly into a sausage shape and place each one lengthwise on a sheet of baking paper. Roll up and twist the ends, place in a steamer. Repeat for the remaining pieces.

Bring plenty of water to the boil in a saucepan and place the steamer on top of this. Steam for 40 minutes. Remove the sausages from the baking paper when you want to use them and sauté in some oil (frying is traditional, but grilling or broiling are also options). Sausages can be refrigerated for up to a week after steaming or frozen for a few months before steaming.

*If using tamari or miso, reduce the salt by half.

seitan roulade with root vegetable stuffing

A celebration-worthy seitan centrepiece for a roast meal. The stuffing is really unique and tasty. It's grain-free, so people on gluten-free or grain-free diets could use this instead as stuffing for a nut roast or lentil loaf. With this recipe it's possible to have an impressive meal to serve to guests in under an hour. It can also be made ahead of and stored in the fridge until baking.

Soy-Free Option
Onion- and Garlic-Free
Under 45 Minutes
Kitchen time 15-20 minutes
Baking time 27 minutes
Serves 4

ingredients

For the seitan:

Dry ingredients:

1 1/2 cups gluten (vital wheat gluten)
1/3 cup chickpea flour
2 tablespoons nutritional yeast (savoury yeast flakes)
1 teaspoon salt (reduce if using tamari or miso)

Wet ingredients:

3 tablespoons vegan worcestershire sauce, tamari, miso or coconut aminos
2 tablespoons oil (olive, sesame, melted coconut or sunflower)
1 1/4 cups water

For the stuffing:

2 cups finely diced parsley root, celery root or parsnip
1/2 cup hazelnut meal or almond meal
2 tablespoons dijon mustard (or 2 teaspoons yellow mustard powder plus 2 tablespoons water)
2 tablespoon fresh thyme, or 2 teaspoons dried
optional 4 tablespoons finely chopped fresh parsley
optional pinch of salt and 1 teaspoon apple cider vinegar (add if using mustard powder instead of mustard)

method

Preheat the oven to 175c (350f).

To make the seitan, combine the dry ingredients in a mixing bowl. Combine the wet ingredients in a separate bowl, then add to the dry mixture, stirring, then kneading to combine. Leave to rest for at least 5 minutes.

Prepare your side dish and stuffing ingredients while the seitan rests and the oven heats up.

Grease a baking sheet and stretch the seitan out into as large a rectangle as you can without it breaking. Place on the sheet and continue to press it out until it gets bigger, without it breaking. It should be less than 1cm (1/2" thick).

Brush the top with oil and bake for 7 minutes. Remove from the oven.

Bring a tiny amount of water to the boil in a small pot, then add the parsley root and boil for 5 minutes. Drain.

In a small bowl, mix the parsley root, hazelnut meal, mustard, thyme and parsley together.

Place the least browned side of the seitan down on a plate and place the parsley root mixture in the middle third of the rectangle. Roll the shorter end towards the other shorter end of the rectangle, overlapping it a little bit to completely cover the filling. Tie it up with cotton string and stuff any of the fallen-out stuffing back inside it. Leave it seam-side down until you're ready to cook it.

When your roasted veggies have 20 minutes to go, place the seitan on the same tray as them, or a separate greased tray, and brush liberally with oil. Bake for 20 minutes. Best served with gravy.

87

side dishes

oven chips

Gluten-Free, Soy-Free, No Specialty Ingredients, Low Fat, Nightshade-Free Option
Onion- and Garlic-Free
No Nuts, Under 45 Minutes
Kitchen time 5-10 minutes
Baking time 30-50 minutes
Serves 2

Following these directions will get you perfect golden chips that are crispy on the outside, and fluffy on the inside. If you don't have the time to turn the chips over at 20 minutes, you can just give the tray a shake (to make the chips move around and flip over) and that will suffice.

ingredients

400g-500g (14-18oz) potatoes or sweet potatoes
2-3 teaspoons cooking oil
4-7 pinches of salt (a small sprinkle, you can add more later if you like)

method

Preheat the oven to 400f (375c)

Peel the sweet potatoes, if using.

Cut the potatoes or sweet potatoes into slices as thick or thin as you would like, then slice again, into chip shapes all around the same size. It's best to have thicker chips, rather than thin, because thinner ones tend to get overcooked very quickly.

Place on a baking sheet with the oil, and flip them around in it, making sure they're all coated. Move them around so that none are touching, then sprinkle with the salt.

Bake for 20 minutes, then shake the tray. For best results quickly flip over every chip so that the less cooked sides are now touching the baking sheet.

Bake for another 10-30 minutes (the time will depend on the size of your chips), then test one of the larger chips to see if it is cooked on the inside.

Variation: For spicy chips, you can sprinkle these with 2 or more pinches of cayenne pepper, and a few pinches of paprika before baking.

Gluten-Free, Soy-Free, No Specialty Ingredients
Low Fat, Nightshade-Free, Onion- and Garlic-Free
No Nuts, Under 45 Minutes
Kitchen time 5 minutes
Cooking time 25-30 minutes
Serves 2

ginger and sesame rice

A quick and easy way to flavour rice that compliments many Asian dishes, especially salt and pepper tofu (page 47).

ingredients

1 tablespoon sesame seeds
3/4 cup brown rice
1 tablespoon finely chopped fresh ginger
1 1/4 cups cold water

method

In a small dry saucepan, toast the sesame seeds over a medium-high heat, stirring constantly until lightly toasted. Set aside for later.

Rinse the rice and place it in the saucepan with the ginger and water. Bring to the boil, reduce the heat and simmer with the lid on for 25-30 minutes. Take off the heat and set aside for 5 minutes.

Place the rice in a serving dish or separate plates and sprinkle with the toasted sesame seeds, to serve.

spicy vegetable broth

Gluten-Free Option, Soy-Free Option,
No Specialty Ingredients
Low Fat, No Nuts, Under 45 Minutes
Kitchen time 5-10 minutes
Cooking time 2-10 minutes
Serves 4

A warming broth that is a great side dish for many Asian meals, or as a drink on its own to help heal colds and flus. To make this higher in protein, add some peas, beans or sprouts.

ingredients

1 spring onion (green onion), chopped
2 tablespoons finely chopped fresh ginger
3 cloves garlic, finely chopped
5 teaspoons minced chili, or 1/2 - 1 teaspoon cayenne pepper, to taste
4 cups water
1 heaped dinner plate fast cooking vegetables
(eg. carrot, broccoli, cabbage, kale, bok choy)
3 tablespoons miso
2 tablespoons apple cider vinegar or lemon juice

method

In a medium-sized saucepan, sauté the spring onion for a couple of minutes, until tender and fragrant, then stir through the ginger, garlic and minced chili for another 30-60 seconds. Add the water and vegetables and bring to the boil. Reduce the heat and simmer until the vegetables are cooked, around 2-10 minutes. Take off the heat and stir through the miso and vinegar.

crispy garlic toast

Gluten-Free, Soy-Free, No Specialty Ingredients, Nightshade-Free
No Nuts, Under 45 Minutes
Total time 5-10 minutes
Serves 2

An easy and tasty way to revive old bread, for serving with soups, Italian dishes and more.

ingredients

4 cloves garlic
a pinch of salt
4 teaspoons coconut oil (or other cooking oil)
7 thin slices homemade bread
optional 1 teaspoon nutritional yeast
(savoury yeast flakes)

method

Crush the garlic with the salt in a mortar and pestle (or chop the garlic very finely). Mix through the coconut oil and nutritional yeast.

If grilling (broiling), first grill one side of the bread, flip over, spread with the garlic oil and cook until crispy and golden.

If baking, place the bread slices on a baking sheet, spread with the garlic oil and bake for around 10 minutes, until crispy and golden.

roasted vegetables

Gluten-Free, Soy-Free, No Specialty Ingredients, Low Fat Option
Nightshade-Free Option, Onion- and Garlic-Free Option
No Nuts, Under 45 Minutes Option
Kitchen time 5-10 minutes

To master the art of delicious roasted vegetables, and co-ordinate them with the rest of a meal there are a few things to understand:

1. The bigger the veggie pieces, the less chance there is of them being overcooked if they need to wait in the oven while the rest of the meal finishes cooking.
2. To make all the roasted veggies at once, keep the pieces around the same size as each other; otherwise you can start some earlier, and others later.
3. Always taste-test one of the slightly larger pieces when you think it may be ready, to make sure it's cooked to perfection.
4. The veggies benefit from being shaken or flipped after 20-30 minutes of cooking, to help brown them more evenly.
5. Beetroot takes longer than other veggies to cook, so chop it up smaller, or begin roasting it earlier than the other vegetables.

vegetables that roast well

Cauliflower is incredible - cut it into pieces around the same size and make sure these get thoroughly cooked through and browned on the edges - 45 minutes for larger florets, 30 minutes for smaller ones
Potatoes
Sweet Potatoes
Carrots
Onions (be gentle with these if they've been chopped up - don't toss with the other vegetables but instead place straight on the tray, drizzle with a little oil and sprinkle with a tiny amount of salt before baking. If they're scattered around the tray in small pieces they will burn before the other vegetables are cooked)
Leeks
Pumpkin and Winter Squash
Parsnips
Swedes (Rutabagas)
Parsley Root
Celery Root
Beetroot
Tomatoes
Capsicum (Peppers)
Zucchini (Courgette/Summer Squash)
Kale tossed with some oil and a tiny pinch of salt added for the last 10 minutes of cooking will result in crispy, delicious chips

method

Cut vegetables into pieces around the same size. Place on a baking sheet or tray with some oil (preferably olive or refined coconut), around 1-4 teaspoons for every serve, and toss them around in the oil to coat. Lightly sprinkle with salt (you can add more later) and bake for 20-30 minutes before shaking the tray or turning each individual piece over to brown a new side. Bake until thoroughly cooked through - another 10-40 minutes, depending on the size of the pieces.

garlic quinoa

A tasty way to serve quinoa - it tastes like garlic bread.

ingredients

Gluten-Free, Soy-Free
No Specialty Ingredients
Low Fat, Nightshade-Free
No Nuts, Under 45 Minutes
Kitchen time 5 minutes
Cooking time 15 minutes
Serves 2

3/4 cup quinoa
1 1/2 cups water
1 clove garlic, finely chopped
half a teaspoon of salt (or to taste)
1-2 teaspoons olive oil
optional 1-2 tablespoons finely chopped fresh parsley

method

Rinse the quinoa under lukewarm water by placing it in a bowl, filling the bowl with water and mixing the quinoa with your fingers, to try and remove as much of the bitter-tasting coating as possible. Drain, and repeat the rinsing at least twice, then drain again. For best results soak the quinoa in some fresh cold water for at least an hour (preferably 12-24 hours), then drain and place in a small saucepan with 1 1/2 cups of water.

Bring to the boil. Reduce heat and simmer for 15 minutes with the lid on, then take off the heat and leave to sit for 5-10 minutes. Stir through the garlic, salt, olive oil and parsley until evenly mixed. Serve hot.

dips, sauces and other condiments

baba ghannouj

Gluten-Free, Soy-Free, No Specialty Ingredients, No Nuts, Under 45 Minutes Option
Kitchen time 5-10 minutes
Baking time 25-45 minutes

A delicious eggplant-based dip that seems to please even eggplant haters! This goes really well served with baked dolmathes (page 62), pictured opposite, as a dip with raw veggies or pita bread, or as a sandwich spread with some mashed chickpeas and salad leaves.

ingredients

700g eggplants (1.5lb)
1/4 cup lemon juice
2-4 tablespoons tahini
2 cloves garlic
salt, to taste (I use 1 -1 1/2 teaspoons)

method

Prick the eggplants all over with a fork and place directly on the oven rack in a preheated oven (around 400f/200c) until soft, with wrinkled skin. This takes 25-30 minutes for the thin Lebanese and Japanese eggplants, or 45 minutes for the traditional large oval ones. Remove from oven and leave until cold enough to handle. Remove the skin, place the pulp in a food processor, along with the lemon juice, tahini, garlic and salt, and process until fairly smooth.

chermoula

Gluten-Free, Soy-Free, No Specialty Ingredients
No Nuts, Under 45 Minutes
Total time 15 minutes
Serves 4-6 as a baked tofu marinade

My version of the zesty garlic, spice, herb and lemon-based North African condiment. Great for baking soy-free tofu, drizzling over the top of vegetables, grains and beans, or using as a sauce in a wrap.

ingredients

2 1/2 teaspoons cumin seeds
1 1/2 teaspoons coriander seeds
7 cloves garlic, peeled
3/4 teaspoon salt
3/4 teaspoon paprika
optional pinch of cayenne pepper
zest and juice of 1 1/2 lemons
1/3 cup olive oil
1/3 cup water
1 1/2 cups fresh coriander leaves(cilantro), parsley or a mix of the two, finely chopped

method

In a dry saucepan or frying pan, toast the cumin and coriander seeds over medium heat, shaking often until they smell toasted, a couple of minutes. Crush in a mortar and pestle (if using), then add the garlic and salt and crush until no large pieces of garlic remain (if you don't have a mortar and pestle, just chop the garlic very finely instead and grind the spices in a spice grinder or food processor).

Combine all the ingredients in a mixing bowl and whisk with a fork to combine.

To bake tofu in the chermoula, cut the tofu into whatever shapes you wish. On a lined baking sheet, place a little chermoula under each tofu shape, place the tofu on top, and cover it with more chermoula. Repeat for the rest of the shapes. Bake for 25-40 minutes, serve right away, or cool and use for salads and snacks.

cashew mayonnaise

Gluten-Free, Soy-Free, No Specialty Ingredients
Nightshade-Free, Onion- and Garlic-Free
Under 45 Minutes
Kitchen time 3 minutes

ingredients

1 cup raw cashews
1 cup water
1 tablespoon apple cider vinegar
1/4 cup vegan milk
1/4 - 1/2 cup olive oil
salt and pepper to taste (I use around half a teaspoon of each)

method

In a blender, soak the cashews in the water and vinegar for at least a couple of minutes, or up to 12 hours. Blend until smooth, then blend in the vegan milk. Slowly drizzle in the olive oil while blending. Add salt and pepper to taste. This will keep in the fridge for up to a week.

93

cashew cheeze

Gluten-Free, Soy-Free
Nightshade-Free, Onion- and Garlic-Free
No Nuts Option, Under 45 Minutes
Kitchen time 3 minutes

This makes a thick cheesy spread that's perfect for spreading on bread for burgers, using on pizzas or making a quick meal of grilled cheese and kale on toast.

ingredients

3/4 cup cashews, sunflower seeds or almonds
1/2 cup water
1/2 cup nutritional yeast (savoury yeast flakes)
1 teaspoon apple cider vinegar
optional 1 teaspoon agave
1/2 teaspoon salt

method

For best results, soak the cashews in the water before blending for as little as a few minutes or as long as 12 hours.

In a blender or food processor, combine all the ingredients on a low setting. Increase the speed to the highest setting after 20 seconds then blend for another 2 minutes or so, until smooth. This will thicken in the fridge.

hummus

Gluten-Free, Soy-Free, No Specialty Ingredients
Nightshade-Free Option, Onion- and Garlic-Free Option
No Nuts, Under 45 Minutes
Total time 5 minutes

High in protein from chickpeas and tahini, with a delicious taste and texture, this hummus is great as a dip or for use in sandwiches and wraps. If you're after a really creamy, restaurant-style hummus, use only around a cup of the chickpeas, otherwise it's still delicious using the full 1 1/2 cups.

ingredients

1/3 cup tahini
1/6 cup lemon juice or apple cider vinegar
1/6 cup water
1 clove garlic, optional
salt, to taste (around 1/2-1 teaspoon)
1 teaspoon cumin
optional cayenne pepper, to taste
1 1/2 cups cooked chickpeas
optional 1 teaspoon paprika, for sprinkling on top

method

Combine the tahini, lemon juice and garlic in a food processor. Blend until creamy, then mix in the salt, cumin and cayenne pepper. Add the chickpeas and blend until combined. This makes a very thick hummus, and may need to be stirred a couple of times to get the chickpeas to blend in.

Place in a serving dish, drizzle with olive oil if you wish and sprinkle with paprika.

mushroom gravy

Gluten-Free, Soy-Free
No Specialty Ingredients, Nightshade-Free
No Nuts, Under 45 Minutes
Kitchen time 10 minutes
Serves 4

A delicious and hearty gravy - perfect with baked seitan and oven chips (for baked seitan, just make the seitan roulade mix (page 87), divide it into 4 'steaks', drizzle with oil and bake for 25-30 minutes, flipping over halfway through)

ingredients

2 tablespoons olive oil, or other cooking oil
1 medium-large onions, finely chopped
250g (9oz) mushrooms (preferably brown ones), sliced
3 tablespoons wholegrain flour of your choice
4 cups water
salt and pepper, to taste

method

Heat the oil in a chef's pan or large saucepan over medium-high heat. Sauté the onions in the oil until tender and fragrant - around 5 minutes, then stir through the mushrooms for another 3-4 minutes. Stir through the flour, then add the water. Bring to the boil, reduce the heat and simmer for at least ten minutes. Add salt and pepper, to taste.

miso gravy

Gluten-Free Option, Soy-Free Option,
No Specialty Ingredients, Low Fat
Nightshade-Free, No Nuts, Under 45 Minutes
Kitchen time 10 minutes
Serves 4

Another delicious gravy, this one is flavoured with miso and herbs.

ingredients

1 medium onion
4 tablespoons flour (whole barley, spelt, wheat or gluten-free)
2 cups water
3 tablespoons miso
3/4 teaspoon dried thyme
1/4 teaspoon dried sage
1/4 teaspoon dried rosemary
cracked pepper, to taste
1/2 teaspoon balsamic vinegar

method

Place the onion in a frying pan with a little olive oil, stirring to coat. Put on a medium-high heat and continue to stir until the onions are tender and fragrant and starting to brown. Stir through the flour, then stir through the water, a little at a time so that no lumps form. Add the miso, herbs, pepper and vinegar and bring to the boil. Reduce heat and simmer for at least 5 minutes.

arugula (rocket) pesto

Gluten-Free Option, Soy-Free Option,
No Specialty Ingredients
Nightshade-Free, Onion- and Garlic-Free
No Nuts, Under 45 Minutes
Total time 5 minutes

ingredients

1/4 cup pumpkin seeds, preferably toasted
1 tablespoon mellow light miso or nutritional yeast
a pinch of salt (add an extra pinch of using nutritional yeast)
1 1/2 packed cups arugula (rocket)
3 tablespoons olive oil
2 tablespoons water

method

Process the pumpkin seeds in a food processor until they are in small, fairly even pieces. Add the miso, arugula, olive oil and water. Process until evenly mixed through.

basil pesto

Gluten-Free, Soy-Free
Nightshade-Free, Onion- and Garlic-Free Option
Under 45 Minutes
Total time 5 minutes

ingredients

1/4 cup cashews
2 teaspoons nutritional yeast
1 clove of garlic (optional)
1/2 teaspoon salt
1/2 teaspoon cracked pepper
1.75oz (50g) fresh basil
3 tablespoons olive oil or water

method

In a food processor combine the cashews, nutritional yeast, garlic, salt and pepper. Process until the cashews are in small, fairly even pieces. Add the basil and olive oil, process until evenly mixed through.

cashew cream

Gluten-Free, Soy-Free, No Specialty Ingredients
Nightshade-Free, Onion- and Garlic-Free
Under 45 Minutes
Kitchen time 3 minutes

Great for adding to soups, curries and other savoury dishes that need extra creaminess, and for serving with desserts. Reducing the amount of water and soaking the cashews for longer will result in a thicker cream.

ingredients

1 cup cashews
1 cup water

For cashew sour cream, add:
3/4 teaspoon salt
1/2 teaspoon agave (optional)
3-6 teaspoons apple cider vinegar or lemon juice

method

For best results, soak the cashews in the water before blending for as little as a few minutes or as long as 12 hours.

In a blender or food processor, combine the cashews and water on a low setting. Increase the speed to the highest setting after 20 seconds then blend for another 2 minutes or so, until smooth. This will thicken in the fridge.

tahini sauce

Gluten-Free, Soy-Free, No Specialty Ingredients
Nightshade-Free, No Nuts, Under 45 Minutes
Total time 5 minutes

ingredients

1/3 cup tahini
1-3 cloves of garlic, finely chopped
optional handful of parsley, finely chopped
a pinch of salt
a pinch of ground cumin
1/6 cup lemon juice or apple cider vinegar
1/6 cup water
1 tablespoon olive oil

method

Put the tahini, garlic, parsley, salt and cumin in a bowl, slowly add the lemon juice and water, whisking with a fork to combine. Don't worry if it doesn't mix well straight away, more whisking will do the trick. Whisk through the oil and serve.

pepperoni beans

Gluten-Free, Soy-Free, Low Fat, No Nuts
Under 45 Minutes
Kitchen time 3 minutes

An easy way to add protein and flavour to pizzas, pizza toast and calzones.

ingredients

1 1/2 cups cooked adzuki beans (or borlotti, or pinto)
2 teaspoons smoked paprika
1/2 - 1 teaspoon ground black pepper
cayenne pepper, to taste
3 cloves of garlic, finely chopped
miso or salt, to taste

method

Mash the beans in a bowl and stir through the rest of the ingredients. Add as an ingredient on pizzas, calzones or pizza toast with mushrooms, olives, pineapple and cashew cheeze and bake or grill (broil) until hot.

lemon cheezecake

A creamy lemon filling reminiscent of lemon meringue pie with the option of a berry topping, on a perfect just-sweet-enough cheezecake base.

Gluten-Free, Soy-Free
Nightshade-Free, Onion- and Garlic-Free
Kitchen time: 10 minutes
Cashew soaking time: 30 minutes-12 hours
Cake setting time: at least 2 hours

ingredients

For the filling:
2 cups raw cashews, soaked in water for at least half an hour (preferably 8-12 hours) and drained
zest of 2 1/2 lemons
2/3 cup lemon juice (around 3-4 lemons)
1/3 cup coconut oil, liquid
1/3 cup raw agave syrup
a pinch of salt

For the base:
1 1/2 cups almonds, walnuts or pecans
a pinch of salt
4 medjool dates, pitted
1/3 cup coconut oil, liquid

Optional berry topping:
3/4 cup berries, fresh or frozen (I use blueberries)
2 teaspoons raw agave syrup (optional)
3 tablespoons water
1 tablespoon chia seeds (optional, for a more gelled topping)

method

For the base:
Process the almonds and salt in a food processor until crumbly, but not too fine (some will resemble almond meal, and some will be more like the nut pieces that go into pesto). Add the dates and process until no large pieces remain. Process through the coconut oil until evenly mixed in. Press the mixture into a greased or lined 8" (20cm) springform pan.

For the lemon filling:
Soak the cashews, then drain. Place in a blender with the other ingredients and blend until smooth. You may need to stop blending and mix through with a spoon from time to time.

If you're having a lot of trouble blending add a tablespoon or two of water and blend until smooth. Pour the blended mixture over the top of the crust.

For the berry topping:
Place the berries in a bowl and mix through the agave, water and chia seeds, if using. Leave to stand for at least 15 minutes, then blend until smooth. If you have fresh berries you can just decorate the top of the cheezecake with these instead of making the topping.

Spread on top of the lemon filling and leave to set in the fridge or freezer for at least two hours. This cake will keep well in the fridge for a week.

chocolate custard

All the delicious taste of a chocolate custard but with extra nutrition, including lots of essential fatty acids from the chia seeds.

Gluten-Free,
Nightshade-Free, Onion- and Garlic-Free
Under 45 Minutes
Kitchen time: 2 minutes
Total time: 5-10 minutes
Makes 1 large or 2 small serves

ingredients

1/2 cup cashews
2-3 tablespoons chia seeds
3 dates, pitted
3 tablespoons cacao or cocoa powder
1 cup water
one frozen banana*
a pinch of salt
optional tiny pinch of vanilla bean pulp

method

Place all ingredients in the blender and leave to sit for a few minutes, for the cashews, dates, chia seeds and banana to soften. Blend until smooth and serve right away.

*Peel bananas and break into chunks, then freeze in bags or containers for use in this recipe, along with the ice cream recipes from this book.

99

chocolate ice cream

A delicious chocolate ice cream, made really quickly without an ice cream machine. From tasting this treat you would never guess that the base ingredient is bananas - it is so creamy and chocolaty - similar to a chocolate gelato.

Gluten-Free, Soy-Free, No Specialty Ingredients
Nightshade-Free, Onion- and Garlic-Free
No Nuts Option, Under 45 Minutes
Total time: 2-5 minutes
Makes 1 large or 2 small serves

ingredients

2 frozen bananas
3 tablespoons cacao or cocoa powder
2 teaspoons agave or maple syrup
2 tablespoons nut butter (preferably almond or hazelnut, use coconut butter for a nut-free option)
4 tablespoons vegan milk
optional tiny scrape of vanilla bean pulp
optional 1 tablespoon chia or hemp seeds

method

Combine all the ingredients in a food processor or blender. Process until smooth, scraping the sides down and mixing it in several times to ensure even blending. This is best eaten right away, but will keep in the freezer for later.

peanut butter choc chip ice cream

A chocolate-speckled treat full of nutty flavour. As with the chocolate ice cream above, this recipe is not one you would suspect is based on bananas. Hemp seeds are great in place of the peanut butter for a nut-free option with more essential fatty acids.

Gluten-Free, Soy-Free, No Specialty Ingredients
Nightshade-Free, Onion- and Garlic-Free
No Nuts Option, Under 45 Minutes
Total time: 2-5 minutes
Makes 1 large or 2 small serves

ingredients

2 frozen bananas
3 tablespoons peanut butter or hemp seeds
4 tablespoons vegan milk
optional tiny scrape of vanilla bean pulp
15g (0.5oz) raw chocolate (or regular vegan chocolate), broken into small pieces

method

Combine the bananas, peanut butter, vegan milk and vanilla bean pulp in a food processor or blender. Process until smooth, scraping the sides down and mixing it in several times to ensure even blending. Process through the chocolate until evenly mixed. This is best eaten right away, but will keep in the freezer for later.

caramel sundae

A refreshing treat with banana-based soft-serve ice cream, caramel sauce and nutritious hemp seeds. If you don't have hemp seeds, any kind of nut crushed into small pieces can be substituted.

Gluten-Free, Low Fat
Nightshade-Free, Onion- and Garlic-Free
No Nuts, Under 45 Minutes
Total time: 5 minutes
Makes 1 large or 2 small serves

ingredients

2 frozen bananas
4 tablespoons vegan milk
optional tiny scrape of vanilla bean pulp

dark agave syrup, for drizzling
hemp seeds or crushed up nuts for sprinkling

method

Combine the bananas, vegan milk and vanilla pulp in a food processor or blender. Process until smooth, scraping the sides down and mixing several times to ensure even blending.

Place in a serving dish, drizzle with agave and sprinkle with hemp seeds.

chocolate fudge

Decadent-tasting melt-in-your-mouth homemade chocolate treats that take minimal kitchen time to make and keep well in the freezer for up to a few months.

Gluten-Free,
Nightshade-Free, Onion- and Garlic-Free
No Nuts option
Kitchen time: 5 minutes
Setting time: 1 hour

ingredients

1/3 cup raw cacao or cocoa powder
a pinch or two of salt
optional tiny scrape of vanilla bean pulp
1/2 cup melted coconut oil
1/4 cup brazil nut butter, almond butter, hazelnut butter, cashew butter or coconut butter
1/3 - 1/2 cup dark raw agave syrup

method

Combine the cacao, salt and vanilla pulp in a mixing bowl. In a measuring cup or separate bowl, combine the coconut oil with the nut butter and 1/3 cup of agave. Stir the wet ingredients into the cacao bowl and add more spoonfuls of agave, to taste. Place in a lined dish and refrigerate until set (around an hour). Cut into small pieces and enjoy right away, or store in the fridge or freezer for later. Alternatively this can be enjoyed at room temperature as a fudge sauce for vegan ice cream, or an icing for cakes.

chocolate chip biscuits

A chocolate chip biscuit without all the hassle of mixing and baking - and it's even more delicious than the baked version. These raw biscuits are a light-caramel flavoured dough with just the right amount of sweetness, speckled with raw chocolate pieces. Just combine a few healthy ingredients in a food processor and you can enjoy this straight away with a spoon in 5-10 minutes, or make it into shapes to serve later.

Gluten-Free,
Nightshade-Free, Onion- and Garlic-Free
Under 45 Minutes
Total time 15-20 minutes

ingredients

1 1/2 cups almonds
1/8 teaspoon salt
optional 1/8 teaspoon cinnamon
7 dates
2 tablespoons coconut oil, liquid
1 oz (30g) raw chocolate, broken into smaller pieces

method

In a food processor combine the almonds, salt and cinnamon. Process until finely ground.

Add the dates and coconut oil and continue to process until minimal traces of dates remain. Add the chocolate and process until evenly mixed through (the pieces should be around the same size as chocolate chips).

Shape the mixture with your hands into any shape you like. Enjoy right away, or keep in the fridge for up to a week.

caramel slice

A raw vegan version of an old favourite with a chewy caramel filling and thin chocolate topping, this slice is delicious and tastes a little bit like caramel nougat chocolate bars, only better. It can be made as a slice in a square pan, or as a torte in a round springform tin. For best results use almonds for the base, although walnuts or pecans will also make a great slice.

Gluten-Free, Soy-Free
Nightshade-Free, Onion- and Garlic-Free
Under 45 minutes
Kitchen time 10-15 minutes
Setting time: 30-60 minutes

ingredients

For the base:
1 1/2 cups almonds, walnuts or pecans
a pinch of salt
4 medjool dates, pitted
1/3 cup coconut oil, liquid

For the caramel filling:
18 medjool dates, pitted
2-3 pinches of salt
1/4 cup coconut oil, liquid
1/4 cup nut butter (hazelnut, almond, cashew or brazil nut)

For the chocolate topping:
1/4 cup coconut oil, liquid
a pinch of salt
2-3 tablespoons raw agave syrup
1/2 cup cacao or cocoa powder

method

To make the base, process the almonds and salt in a food processor until crumbly, but not too fine (some will resemble almond meal, and some will be more like the nut pieces that go into pesto). Add the dates and process until no large pieces remain. Process through the coconut oil until evenly mixed in. Press the mixture into a greased or lined 20cm (8") square or round baking tray.

To make the caramel layer, process the dates and salt in a food processor until it is finely ground and forms a ball. Add the coconut oil and nut butter and continue to process until thoroughly mixed through (you may need to stop the processor and break up the ball with a fork a couple of times). Press this mixture into an even layer on top of the base.

Prepare the chocolate topping by combining the coconut oil, salt and agave in a bowl. Stir through the cacao and mix until evenly combined, adding more agave if you like. Spread this on top of the caramel layer (you may need to use your hands to spread it) and allow to set at room temperature for at least half an hour before slicing, or until the chocolate topping has set.

chocolate mousse cake

A decadent-tasting chocolate mousse cake, with the optional addition of cherries.

Gluten-Free,
Nightshade-Free, Onion- and Garlic-Free
Kitchen time 10-15 minutes
Total time: 3-13 hours

ingredients

For the mousse:

1/2 cup (packed) dried cherries (100g/3.5oz) or dates
3 cups raw cashews
water, for soaking
1/4 teaspoon salt
3/4 cup coconut oil, liquid
1/2 - 3/4 cup raw agave syrup (use only 1/2 cup, if using dates instead of cherries)
1 cup reserved cherry soaking water
1 cup raw cacao (or cocoa)

For the base:

1 1/2 cups almonds, walnuts or pecans
1/4 cup raw cacao or cocoa powder
a pinch of salt
7 medjool dates, pitted
1/2 cup coconut oil, liquid

For the optional cherry sauce:

1/2 cup (packed) dried cherries (100g/3.5oz)
3/4 cup water

method

Soak the cashews and cherries or dates for the mousse in separate bowls for at least an hour, preferably 8 hours. Drain the cashews. Reserve one cup of the cherry-soaking water.

For the base, process the almonds, cacao and salt in a food processor until crumbly, but not too fine (some will resemble almond meal, and some will be more like the nut pieces that go into pesto). Add the dates and process until no large pieces remain. Process through the coconut oil until evenly mixed in. Press the mixture into a greased or lined 20cm (8") or 23cm (9") springform pan.

To make the filling, combine the soaked cherries or dates, cashews, salt, coconut oil, agave syrup and cherry-soaking water in a blender and process until smooth. Blend through the cacao and pour over the prepared base.

If using the cherries, for a marble effect you could pour out 1/3 of the mixture before the cacao is added into a separate bowl, then add the cacao to the rest. Pour in small layers onto the base and swirl with a fork to create the marble effect.

Refrigerate for at least 5 hours, or freeze for two hours.

To make the cherry sauce, combine the cherries and water in a blender (for best results leave them to soak for at least a few minutes before blending). Blend until fairly smooth, then strain through a nutmilk bag, cheesecloth or very fine sieve. Drizzle on top of individual slices.

dark chocolate and orange truffles

These truffles are intensely bitter-sweet, for fans of very dark (80% cocoa or higher) chocolate. They are just sweet enough to counter the bitterness of the cacao and orange, so add some more dates if you'd prefer a sweeter truffle.

Gluten-Free,
No Specialty Ingredients Option
Nightshade-Free, Onion- and Garlic-Free
Under 45 Minutes
Total time 15-20 minutes

ingredients

2 cups walnuts
a pinch of salt
22 medjool dates, pitted (or around 2 cups of smaller dates)
1 cup cacao or cocoa powder
1 cup almonds
finely grated zest and juice of one orange

method

In a food processor, grind the walnuts until floury (be careful not to over-process them, or they will turn into walnut butter). Add the dates and process until evenly combined and minimal traces of dates remain. Add the cacao and almonds and process until the almonds are in very small pieces. Add the orange zest and juice and process until evenly mixed through.

Take teaspoons of the mixture and roll into balls, coating each one in cacao, hulled hemp seeds, desiccated coconut or finely chopped nuts.

Serve these right away, or keep them in the fridge for up to a week.

halva

This is a Greek-style vanilla halva made from sesame seeds. Raw and homemade, it is much healthier and tastier than the shop-bought stuff.

Gluten-Free,
Nightshade-Free, Onion- and Garlic-Free
No Nuts, Under 45 minutes
Kitchen time: 5-10 minutes

ingredients

1 cup sesame seeds
a pinch of salt
optional pinch of cinnamon
scraped insides from half a vanilla bean
1/4 cup agave syrup
2 tablespoons tahini

For the optional chocolate swirl:
2 tablespoons raw cacao or cocoa powder
2 teaspoons agave syrup

method

Combine the sesame seeds, salt, cinnamon and vanilla bean pulp in a food processor. Process for around 3 minutes, or until very finely ground with no whole seeds remaining. Add the agave and tahini and continue to process until evenly mixed through.

If adding the optional chocolate swirl, transfer 2/3 of the vanilla mixture to a separate bowl. Create the chocolate mixture by adding the cacao and agave to the remaining 1/3 of the mixture and process until mixed through.

Place half of the vanilla mixture on the base of a small container. Top with the chocolate layer, and then the remaining mixture. Use a fork to swirl it around to create a marble effect. Refrigerate until firm and serve as a slice, or roll into small balls.

Gluten-Free, ~~Soy-Free~~, No Specialty Ingredients, Nightshade-Free, Onion- and Garlic-Free, No Nuts option
Under 45 Minutes option
Kitchen time 5 minutes

To make any of these milks, soak the ingredients if required, rinse and drain if you wish, then combine with cold water, a pinch of salt and any supplements such as calcium or vitamin D in a blender. Blend for around a minute, then strain through a nut milk bag or some cheesecloth.

I use nut milk bags with elastic tops that stretch to fit over the top of the blender, straining and pouring the milk at the same time through a large funnel directly into bottles for storage, this can get messy when working with eight cup batches of milks. Other people sometimes use jelly-making bags suspended over mixing bowls, or squeeze the milk from nutmilk bags into a large jug or bowl before pouring into bottles.

The amount of milk to make at one time depends on your households needs, along with blender capacity. I usually make vegan milk in eight cup batches because we use that much in around two days, but smaller households may prefer a four or six cup batch.

Whether to add any sweetener or not to the milks is a personal choice. Shop-bought vegan milks often contain sweeteners, and animal milks contain sugar in the form of lactose, so many people are used to milks that have already been sweetened. I don't think sweeteners are neccessary, but for those who would prefer a sweeter milk I recommend adding one or two pitted dates before blending, or blending through a little agave, to taste.

For extra nutrition try adding a few teaspoons of hemp seeds per 4 cups of water. Half a teaspoon of sea vegetables such as wakame for every four cups of water is also a good addition to any of these milks.

coconut milk

Coconut flakes don't require soaking, so this milk can be made without any notice. There is quite a lot of leftover pulp, and the milk isn't as creamy as nut milks, or as high in protein, but is an essential ingredient in some Asian dishes, and also makes a delicious hot chocolate. This milk doesn't impart too much coconut flavour, so can be used for most purposes, although it doesn't curdle to make vegan buttermilk in the same way that nut milks can.
For every 4 cups of water: 2 cups unsweetened full-fat coconut flakes

cashew milk

The cashews for cashew milk benefit from soaking - even for just a couple of minutes, and for best results should be soaked for 8-12 hours. Cashew milk leaves minimal amounts of leftover pulp, so is good if you don't like to see food go to waste and can't seem to make use of all the pulp that gets left over from making vegan milks, it also means that cashew milk is creamier and richer than vegan milks made from similar amounts of nuts. Great all-purpose milk.
For every 4 cups of water: 1 cup raw unsalted cashews

almond milk

Almonds are one of the highest nuts in calcium. For the creamiest possible milk, and a really decadent-tasting hot chocolate, use one and a half to two cups of nuts for every four cups of water, but milk made from just one cup of almonds is also delicious and makes a good all-purpose vegan milk. Almonds for almond milk should be soaked for 8-12 hours before blending. Great all-purpose milk.
For every 4 cups of water: 1 cup raw unsalted almonds

sunflower seed milk

Sunflower seed milk (at the time of writing this book) is cheaper to make than nut milks, but still offers the same creaminess, high protein and ability to curdle as nut milks. Sunflower seeds for milk should be soaked for 8-12 hours before blending. Great all-purpose milk with minimal leftover pulp.
For every 4 cups of water: 1 cup raw unsalted sunflower seeds

hazelnut milk

Hazelnut milk has a light hazelnut taste that is great for hot chocolate and coffees, and for use in baking and most dishes. Hazelnuts for hazelnut milk should be soaked for 8-12 hours before blending.
For every 4 cups of water: 1 cup of raw unsalted hazelnuts

muesli bars

Delicious and filling nut-free muesli bars that are high in protein, with a hint of cinnamon flavour.

ingredients

3 cups rolled oats
1 cup wholegrain flour (eg. barley, spelt or wheat)
1/2 cup rapadura, or other unrefined sugar
1 1/2 cups sunflower or pumpkin seeds
optional 1/2 cup dried fruit
optional 2 tablespoons chia seeds
1 teaspoon bicarb soda
a pinch of salt
optional 1/2 teaspoon cinnamon
1/2 cup barley malt syrup, warmed
3/4 cup melted coconut oil
1/2 cup water
optional 1 teaspoon vanilla extract

Nightshade-Free
Onion- and Garlic-Free
No Nuts, Under 45 Minutes
Kitchen time: 10 minutes
Total time: 40 minutes

method

Preheat the oven to 350f (175c). Grease or line an 8x12" (20x30cm) baking dish.

Combine the dry ingredients in a mixing bowl.

In a separate bowl combine the barley malt syrup with the coconut oil, water and vanilla. Mix until evenly combined, then add to the dry ingredients. Mix to thoroughly coat, then press into the prepared baking pan.

Bake for around 30 minutes, or until the centre appears to be cooked. Cool before slicing.

hot chocolate

Gluten-Free Option, Soy-Free Option,
No Specialty Ingredients option
Nightshade-Free, Onion- and Garlic Free,
Low Fat, No Nuts option, Under 45 Minutes
Total time 5 minutes
Serves 1

There's no need to buy hot chocolate blends when a delicious hot chocolate can quickly and easily be made at home from better ingredients.

ingredients

1 mug vegan milk
2-3 teaspoons rapadura, sucanat, coconut sugar or other unrefined sugar
1-2 teaspoons cacao or cocoa powder

method

Pour the vegan milk into a saucepan and heat over a medium-high heat, until almost boiling. Take off the heat. Mix the rapadura and cacao in a mug, add a little of the hot vegan milk and thoroughly mix in, then gradually add the rest, stirring with every addition to make sure that it's evenly mixed through.

miso soup in a mug

Gluten-Free Option, Soy-Free Option,
No Specialty Ingredients option
Nightshade-Free, Onion- and Garlic Free,
Low Fat, No Nuts, Under 45 Minutes
Total time 5 minutes
Serves 1

A nourishing and warming broth that is a fantastic snack, and great to sip on if you're hungry and waiting for dinner to cook.

ingredients

1 mug of water
optional teaspoon of small wakame pieces
3-4 teaspoons miso (any kind)

method

Bring 3/4 of the mug of water and the optional wakame to the boil. Take off the heat. Place the miso in a mug and mix in a little cold water, to thin it out. Mix in the hot water and wakame a little at a time and enjoy the drink from the mug.

Some of the miso may settle towards the bottom of the mug. Taking big sips, gently shaking the mug or stirring with a spoon will help to keep it evenly mixed in.

2372216R00062

Made in the USA
San Bernardino, CA
12 April 2013